MUSICANADA 5

Penny Louise Brooks

Betty Anne Kovacs

Mary Martin Trotter

Contributing Author
Doreen Dunne Sunderland

General Editor
Penny Louise Brooks

HOLT, RINEHART AND WINSTON OF CANADA, LIMITED TORONTO.

MUSICANADA 5

Penny Louise Brooks
Independent Consultant, Music and Language Arts
Toronto, Ontario

Betty Anne Kovacs
Music Consultant
Etobicoke Board of Education
Etobicoke, Ontario

Mary Martin Trotter
Music Teacher
Elgin County Board of Education
St. Thomas, Ontario

Doreen Dunne Sunderland
Music Consultant
Renfrew County Board of Ecucation
Pembrooke, Ontario

ISBN 0-03-923180-1

Sponsoring Editor Sheba Meland
Developmental Editor Penny L. Brooks
Art Director Wycliffe Smith
Designer Jim Ireland
Illustrator Maryann Kovalski
Cover Illustration Terry Shoffner

Canadian Cataloguing in Publication Data
Main Entry under title:
Musicanada 5

For use in grade 5.
Includes index.
ISBN 0-03-923180-1

1. School music – Instruction and study – Canada.
2. Music – Instruction and study – Canada – Juvenile.
I. Brooks, Penny, 1950-

MT930.M875   372.8'7049   C82-095037-8

The authors and publisher thank the following educators for contributing valuable commentary during the development of this program:

Margaret Barnes
Music Specialist
Calgary Board of Education
Calgary, Alberta

Barbara Clark
Vocal Music Consultant
Ottawa Board of Education
Ottawa, Ontario

Lorraine Dalgliesh
Music Specialist
Calgary Board of Education
Calgary, Alberta

Peggy Emmond
Music Specialist
St. Boniface School Division #4
Winnipeg, Manitoba

Terry English
Music Consultant
Waterloo County Separate School Board
Kitchener, Ontario

Norine Inkster
Elementary Music Specialist
Calgary Board of Education
Calgary, Alberta

Isabelle Mills
Assistant Dean, College of Arts and Science
University of Saskatchewan
Saskatoon, Saskatchewan

Yvonne Navratil
Music Resource Teacher
Ottawa Board of Education
Ottawa, Ontario

Susan Scott
Music Resource Teacher
Ottawa Board of Education
Ottawa, Ontario

Brenda Trafford
Music Specialist
District 14 School Board
Sackville, New Brunswick

Dennis Tupman
Performing Arts Co-ordinator
Vancouver Board of Education
Vancouver, British Columbia

Rhonda Wicks
Music Co-ordinator
The Avalon Consolidated School Board
St. Johns, Newfoundland

Printed in Canada   9   91

CONTENTS

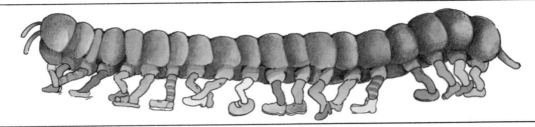

AUTUMN

WINTER

SPRING

AUTUMN

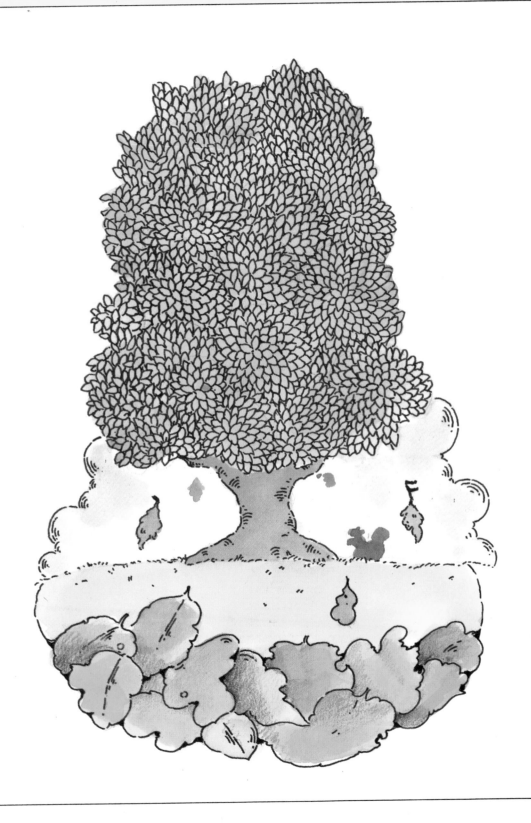

SODIO

Rote Song

Composer Unknown

Music moves with a **steady beat**.
What beat picture matches the beat pattern of this song?
Bounce a ball to the steady beat.

Name the **time signature** that goes with each pattern. How
can you tell which beat gets the **accent**?

D: d' s m d   1 2 3 sing

With spirit

Here we go, so-di-o, so-di-o, so-di-o. Here we go, so-di-o

1. 2.

Fine

all night long!   all night long!   I went to the pla-za, and

what did I see?   A big fat man from Cal-ga - ry.___

I bet-cha five dol-lars I can catch that___ man!

I bet-cha five dol-lars I can catch that___ man!

To the front, to the back, to the see-saw side.

I went to the doc-tor, and what did I say?:___

"Ooh! Ah! I got a pain in my side. Ooh! Ah! I got a

pain in my tum. Ooh! Ah!___ I got a pain in my head."

D.C. al Fine

To the front, to the back, to the see-saw side.

3

MAKE NEW FRIENDS

Eb: d' s m d   1 2 3 sing

Sound is the raw material of music. Pitch is the highness or lowness of sound.
Melodies are made from pitches that move by step, by skip and with repeated notes.
Look at the music to find

this **skip**,   this **stepping**   this **repeated**
                               pattern,   **pattern.**

1   2   3   4

Make new friends, but keep the_ old;_ One is sil - ver and the oth-er gold.

GOT THE RHYTHM? GOT THE BEAT?

BEAT	**Beat** is the steady pulse in music. **Time signatures** tell two things: 2 – the number of beats in a bar, and 4 – the kind of note that gets one beat.

What do these time signatures mean?

$\dfrac{3}{4}$ $\dfrac{6}{8}$ $\dfrac{4}{4}$

ACCENT	**Bar lines** group beats, usually into sets of twos or threes. The first beat of a bar is **accented**.

What **time signatures** go with the following?

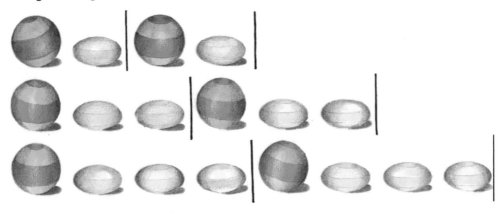

RHYTHM	**Rhythm** has short and long sounds and silences. **Rhythm** may be even or uneven. Review the names and values of the notes in the chart on page 150.

Where do the **bar lines** go in the following phrase?

$\frac{4}{4}$ ♩ ♫ ♫ ♩. ♪♪ ♪ ♫ ♫ ♪ ♩ ♪ ▬

Count and tap the rhythm.
Perform it as you sing "Make New Friends," page 4.

SWINGING ALONG

Rote Song

American

F: *d m s m d s,*   1 2 3 4 1 2 sing

Not all music begins on the strong or accented beat of the bar.
What do you call the note or notes that come before the first strong beat?

Swing-ing a - long _____ the o - pen road,   un-der a

sky that's clear. Swing-ing a - long _____ the o - pen road, in the

fall of the year. Swing-ing a - long, swing-ing a-long, swing-ing a -

long the o - pen road, ___ all in the fall of the year.

MICHAEL FINNIGIN

Note/Rote Song

Irish

G: *d   m   s   m   d   s,*   1   2   1   sing

Use the **doh sign** 𝄐 to find **doh**, the **home tone** of the song.
What syllable is the starting note?

G=doh

1. There was an old man called Mi - chael Fin - ni - gin,
2. There was an old man called Mi - chael Fin - ni - gin,

D7 = soh

He   grew   whis - kers   on   his   chin - i - gin,
He   went   fish - ing   with   a   pin - i - gin,

G

The wind   came   up   and   blew   them   in - i - gin,
Caught   a   fish   but   dropped   it   in - i - gin,

D7   **G**

Poor   old   Mi - chael   Fin - i - gin. (Be - gin - i - gin)
Poor   old   Mi - chael   Fin - i - gin. (Be - gin - i - gin)

3. There was an old man called Michael Finnigin,
Climbed a tree and barked his shinigin,
Took off several yards of skinigin,
Poor old Michael Finnigin. (Beginigin)

4. There was an old man called Michael Finnigin,
He grew fat and then grew thinigin,
Then he died and had to beginigin,
Poor old Michael Finnigin. (Beginigin)

Follow the chord symbols above the song to play an autoharp accompaniment.

7

THE KEEPER

Note/Rote Song

English Folk Song

D: d' s m d m s   1 2 1   sing

Find a place in the music where the class will divide into two groups and sing at different times; together.

What sign in the music tells you where you will divide?

1. The keep-er did a-hunt-ing go, And un-der his cloak
2. The first doe he shot at he missed; The sec-ond doe

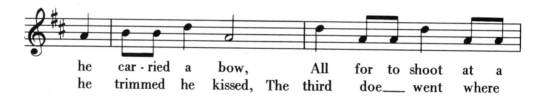

he car-ried a bow, All for to shoot at a
he trimmed he kissed, The third doe___ went where

Chorus

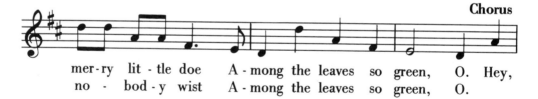

mer-ry lit-tle doe A-mong the leaves so green, O. Hey,
no-bod-y wist A-mong the leaves so green, O.

Jack-ie boy! Sing ye well! Hey, down,

Mas-ter? Ver-y well! Ho, down,

der-ry, der-ry down,   A-mong the leaves so green,   O! To me

A-mong the leaves so green,   O!

hey, down, down,   Hey, down,

To me ho, down, down,   Ho, down,

der-ry, der-ry down,   A-mong the leaves so green,   O!

A-mong the leaves so green,   O!

3. The fourth doe she went o'er the plain,
The keeper fetched her back again;
Where she is now she may remain
Among the leaves so green, O.

4. The fifth doe she did cross the brook;
The keeper fetched her back with his hook;
Where she is now you may go and look
Among the leaves so green, O.

5. The sixth doe she did cross the plain;
But he with his hounds did turn her again,
There they did hunt in a merry, merry vein
Among the leaves so green, O.

WHAT SOUND DO YOU HEAR?

Emily Hearn

Poem

Listen! Listen! What do you hear?
In the room where you are
What comes to your ear?
Listen
Close your eyes . . . now what do you hear?
Outside your room
What comes to your ear?

The crack of a bat socking a homer
The blip, blip, blip of a bouncing ball
The whap, whap of the rope of a skipper
The giggles and shouts
"My turn, you're out!"
The brrrrrrring of the school bell
That ends it all; the shuffle
of footsteps down the hall.

HOPSCOTCH

Play hopscotch. Choose eight squares for your hopscotch route. After square three you have a choice. Where do you make your second decision? Repeat the turning square and hop back again.

Divide into two groups. Choose a different kind of percussion sound for each group to play. Perform the hopscotch in opposite directions at the same time.

10

TEACH ME

Rote Song

Music by R. Toth/Lyrics by J. Sone

These two songs may be sung separately or together as **partner songs**.
Listen to the **harmony** you create when you sing them together.

THE OLD GO-HUNGRY HASH HOUSE

Note/Rote Song

Canadian

C: d' s m d m s   1   2   3   sing

Scales are pitches organized in a certain **pattern**. Collect the pitches from this song and put them on a staff. Arrange them in order from low to high. Play them on the bells.

1. The flap-jacks they were leath-er, they'd stand up in an-y weath-er, You could
2. The sau-sag-es were saw-dust, it -'d make you smile your broad-est, ___To
3. The bis-cuits they were wood-en and we had some cast iron pud-din', ___You

e - ven sew them on as soles for shoes. The syr - up it was paint, if you
hear them claim that they were made of pork! And we nev -er got e -nough, of that
could-n't break the pie-crust with a club. If you weren't a courter of the

smelled it you would faint, And the prunes were dat - ed eight-een - for - ty - nine.
beef that was so tough, You___ could - n't stick the gra - vy with a fork!
land - lad - y's daughter, Oh, you'd nev - er get a de - cent plate of grub.

Chorus

Then we o - pen up the gates, oh we all rush in on roll - er - skates,

In the old Go - Hun - gry Hash House where I board.

12

Pitches may be **organized** to create different scales. Which of these scales did you find in "The Old Go-Hungry Hash House"?

Doh Pentatonic:

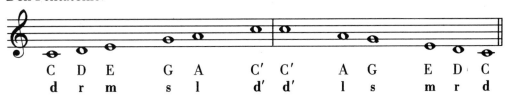

C	D	E		G	A		C′	C′		A	G		E	D	C
d	r	m		s	l		d′	d′		l	s		m	r	d

Major:

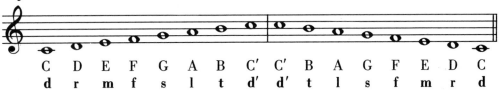

C	D	E	F	G	A	B	C′	C′	B	A	G	F	E	D	C
d	r	m	f	s	l	t	d′	d′	t	l	s	f	m	r	d

Sing each of these scales. Where does each one come to rest?

The **resting note** is called the **home tone**.

What is the **home tone** in each scale?

How are the scales **different**?

MUSIC OF THE RIVER

Note/Rote Song

L. Sweesy and S. Martin

F: d m s m—/d   1   2   1   sing

Where is **doh** in this song?
On what note does the **melody** begin? the **descant**?

Descant

1. Flow - ing, on - ward go;
2. Riv - er, on - ward go;

Melody

1. Gen - tle riv - er, qui - et riv - er, on - ward go.
2. Peace - ful riv - er, no - ble riv - er, broad and strong,

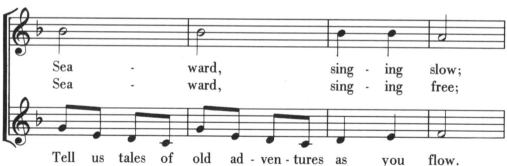

Sea - ward, sing - ing slow;
Sea - ward, sing - ing free;

Tell us tales of old ad - ven - tures as you flow.
Sing a song of no - ble meas - ure, deep and long.

Mur - mur in my dream,_____
Sing sweet songs for me,_____

Tell us tales of new ad - ven - tures yon - der that a - wait,
Stead - y keep your on - ward flow - ing; it shall end - ed be,

14

Songs of long a - go.
Songs of joy to be.

When you pass with sing - ing through the far - off sea-ward gate.
When at last you flow in - to some hap-py, shin-ing sea.

DO NOT WEEP

Note/Rote Song

Ojibwa Melody/Arr. by Keith Bissell

Dm(F): d t, l, d m l   1 2 3 1 2 sing

Songs often begin and end on their **home tone.**
What is the **home tone** in this song?

mf
1. You must not weep, my small one,
2. Morn - ing will bring the sun - shine,

dim.
Dry your eyes now and slum - ber.
Morn - ing will bring the bird - song.

Chorus
mp
Hush - a - bye, hush, my dear one,

dim.
Hear the wind blow-ing in the pine trees.

TEMPO, TEMPO, TEMPO, TEMPO

Bounce a ball to the **steady beat**. Say the chant.

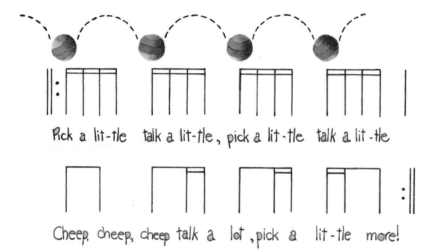

Pick a lit-tle talk a lit-tle, pick a lit-tle talk a lit-tle

Cheep, cheep, cheep talk a lot, pick a lit-tle more!

Sometimes the beat becomes faster or slower.
Change the speed, or **tempo**, of the beat as you bounce and chant.

I AM SLOWLY GOING CRAZY

Rote Song

Camp Song

D: d' s m d   1 2 3 sing

I am slow-ly go-ing cra-zy, one, two, three, four, five, six, switch.

Cra-zy go-ing slow-ly am I, six, five, four, three, two, one, switch.

Divide into two groups. Group 1 sings the song. Group 2 says the chant above. This time, pass and catch the ball on the beat. Increase the tempo. Don't drop the ball!

FINDING DOH WITH FLATS

The **key sign** ⊨ shows where **doh** is.

The group of **sharps** or **flats** placed at the beginning of a line of music is called the **key signature.**

The **key signature** also shows where **doh** is.

When there are **flats** in the key signature, the flat closest to the notes is **fah.**

Count up four steps to high **doh** (**doh'**), or down three steps to **doh.**

In this example, **doh'** is in the 4th space and **doh** is on the 1st line:

Where is **doh** in each of these examples?

Find the music of example 3 in the song "O Give Thanks" on page 18.

EXPRESSION IN THE ARTS

People all over the world celebrate the harvest. It is a time of giving thanks for what the earth provides. How does harvest time make you feel?

Composers, writers and artists often express feelings and moods in their works. What moods have the works on these two pages captured?

The true farmers are laying in the last of their crop now, from the tiny fishing farms of Nova Scotia to the apple valley of the Okanagan and the lush delta of the Fraser River. The countryfolk are heaping up their woodpiles. Small children are examining their skates in the basement. People are wondering where they stored their skis during the summer. In the mountains they are looking to the snowsheds, and on the prairies to the snow fences.

Bruce Hutchinson

O GIVE THANKS

Note Song and Round

Traditional French Melody

Bb: d s, m, d, m, s, d   1 2 1   sing

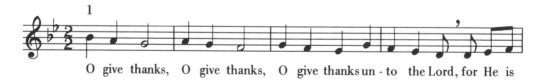

O give thanks, O give thanks, O give thanks un - to the Lord, for He is

gra - cious and His mer - cy en - dur - eth, en - dur - eth for - ev - er.

THE COSSACKS

Note/Rote Song and Round

Ukrainian Folk Melody/Lyrics by J. Wood and B. Kovacs

Dm(F): *d t, l, d m l*   1   2   1   sing

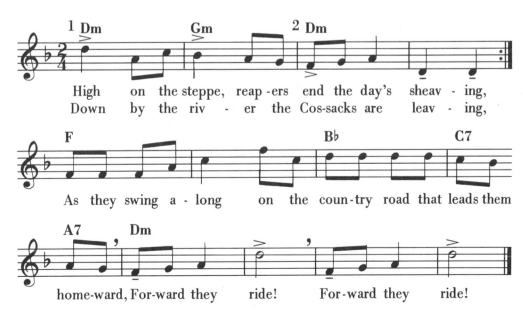

High on the steppe, reap-ers end the day's sheav - ing,
Down by the riv - er the Cos-sacks are leav - ing,

As they swing a - long   on the coun-try road that leads them

home-ward, For-ward they   ride!   For-ward they   ride!

YELLOW SUBMARINE

Rote Song

John Lennon and Paul McCartney

Bounce a steady beat on your desk as you sing:

G: d m s m d m   1 2 3 4 1 2 sing

March tempo

In the town_____ where I was born lived a man_____ who sailed to sea, And he told_____ us of his life in the land_____ of sub - ma - rines. So we sailed_____ up to the sun till we found_____ the sea of green. And we lived_____ be - neath the waves in our yel - low sub - ma - rine.

Words & Music by John Lennon and Paul McCartney. Copyright © 1966 NORTHERN SONGS LIMITED. All Rights for the U.S.A., Canada, Mexico

Chorus

We all live in a yel - low sub - ma - rine,

yel - low sub - ma - rine, yel - low sub - ma - rine,

We all live in a yel - low sub - ma - rine,

yel - low sub - ma - rine, yel - low sub - ma - rine.

And our
As we

friends___ are all on board, man - y more of them live next
live_____ a life of ease, ev - ery one of us___ has all we

1.
2

door. And the band___ be - gins to play . . .
need: Sky of blue_____ and sea of

2.
Repeat Chorus from the 𝄋 and fade

green, in our yel - low sub - ma - rine.

INDEPENDENCE

Rote Song

Pat Patterson and Dodi Robb

Bb: d s, m, d, m, s,   1 2 3 4 1 2 sing

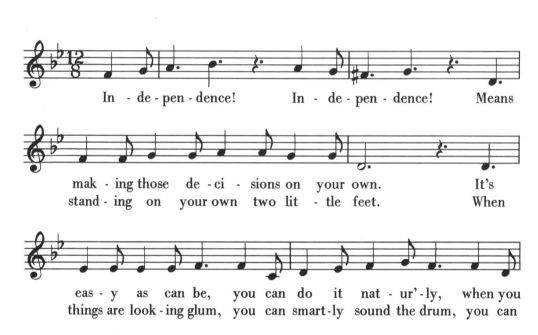

In - de - pen - dence!   In - de - pen - dence!   Means

mak - ing those de - ci - sions on your own.   It's
stand - ing on your own two lit - tle feet.   When

eas - y as can be,   you can do it nat - ur'-ly,   when you
things are look-ing glum, you can smart-ly sound the drum, you can

put to use the things you've al - ways known._____
call the tune and e - ven set the beat._____   A

22

Life's a rock-y riv-er, so pad-dle your own ca-noe.____
team must have a cap-tain and one who knows what to do.____

No-bod-y else can swamp the boat when you're the on-ly crew.
Stick out your chin and tell your-self it might as well be you.

When you're in con-trol and go-ing it a-lone, That's in-de-
When you're cool and not a-fraid to face the heat, That's in-de-

pen - dence. In - de - pen - dence.

HOLY FAMILY SCHOOL

CZECH WALKING SONG

Note Song and Round

Czech Folk Song

1. A - bove the val - ley, fresh and green, the snow - y peaks are
2. And seen by day or eve - ning light, the loft - y peaks give

clear - ly seen. A hu - ya, hu - ya, hu - ya ya,————————
us de - light. swift - ly flow - ing

A hu - ya, hu - ya, hu - ya ya,————————
riv - er, swift - ly flow - ing riv - er.

Leave out the long held notes when you sing
the song as a round.

24

HALLOWEEN

D. Sunderland

Poem

Goblins and ghosts
Gruesome and groaning,
Black witches soaring,
Skeletons moaning.

Creaking and squeaking,
Wild leaves sailing.
Corn stalks hairy,
White ghosts wailing.

Jack-o'-lanterns,
Misty sheen.
Gloomy graveyards,
Halloween!

There are many **sound words** in this poem.

Use different vocal effects to add interest as you say it:
    solo — group
    loud — soft
    whisper echoes
    high — low

What instrumental **colours**, or **timbres**, can you add for special effects?

EXPRESS YOURSELF

Use your voice to change the meaning of these words:
   "Come over here."
Can you make them mean:
   "I like you"?
   "You've been naughty"?

Music can say things, too. The way we perform music helps us
to express its meaning.

Sing "loo" to your favourite tune. By the **expression** in your voice, make it say:

"I am excited."
"I am sad."
"I am angry."
"I am in love."

Which of these expression controls did you vary each time?

Tempo	fast . . . slow
Dynamics	loud . . . soft
Articulation	crisp . . . limp
	staccato . . . legato

HALLOWEEN

Note/Rote Song and Round

J. Wood and H. Behn

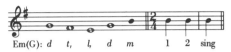

Em(G): *d*   *t,*   *l,*   *d*   *m*   1   2   sing

As you listen, draw a map of how the words are sung. Decide which phrases are
staccato. Decide how you will show *staccato* phrases in your map.
How will you show the *legato* phrases?

1. To - night   is   the night   when   dead   leaves   fly

Like   witch - es   on   switch - es   a - cross   the   sky,

When   elf   and   sprite   flit   through   the   night,

On   a   moon - y   sheen,   on   a   moon - y   sheen.

2. Tonight is the night when leaves do sound
Like gnomes in their homes far beneath the ground,
When spooks and trolls creep out of holes,
Dark and mossy green, dark and mossy green.

WITCHES' CHANT

Text by W. Shakespeare

Arr. by Nancy Telfer

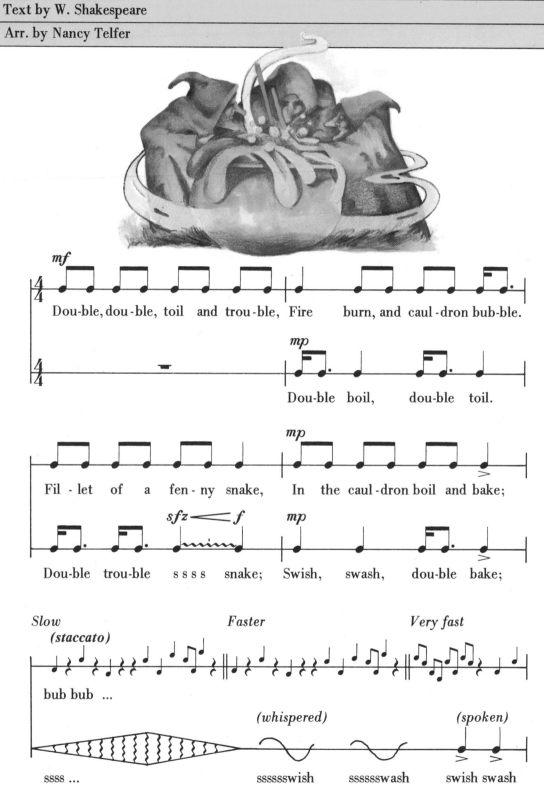

mf
Dou-ble, dou-ble, toil and trou-ble, Fire burn, and caul-dron bub-ble.

mp
Dou-ble boil, dou-ble toil.

Fil-let of a fen-ny snake, *mp* In the caul-dron boil and bake;

Dou-ble trou-ble *sfz* < *f* ssss snake; *mp* Swish, swash, dou-ble bake;

Slow
(staccato)
bub bub ...

Faster

Very fast

(whispered)

(spoken)

ssss ... sssssswish sssssswash swish swash

p (whispered)

Eye of newt, and toe of frog,

mp (spoken)

wool of bat, and tongue of dog:

p (whispered)

Eye of newt, and toe of frog,

mp

H m m m m

Each person chooses a different low note to hum. This sound is called a tone cluster. Then everyone glides upward to form a new tone cluster.

Compose a witches' chant-melody and hum it softly (*legato*). Repeat it, slowly getting louder.

Individuals make up their own boiling sound (*staccato*). Keep changing the tempo.

mf

For a charm of pow-er-ful trou-ble, Like a hell-broth, boil and bub-ble.

mf

Fire burn, Caul-dron bub-ble;

f

p cresc. e accel. - f

Dou-ble, dou-ble, toil and trou-ble, Fire burn, and caul-dron bub-ble!

p cresc. e accel. - f

Fire burn, Fire burn, and caul-dron bub-ble!

29

WITCHES

Rote Song

Traditional/Lyrics by C. Henry

Em(G): *d t, l, d m d l, m,* 1 2 3 4 1 2 sing

Sing this song at different speeds.
Which **tempo** creates a Halloween mood?

1. The moon was lost be-hind a cloud when some-thing weird went by.
2. The stars were gone, the night was dark when some-thing strange took place.

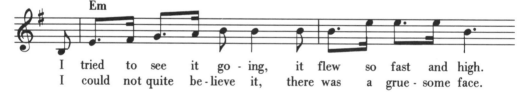

I tried to see it go-ing, it flew so fast and high.
I could not quite be-lieve it, there was a grue-some face.

I don't be-lieve in witch-es, but that is what I saw,
I don't be-lieve in zom-bies, but that is what I saw,

A-sail-ing high up in the sky on a broom-stick of straw.
A skel-e-ton with corpse-like face, ___ I viewed it with awe.

Music uses Italian words to indicate **tempo**. Which of these did you choose?

Adagio — Slowly
Andante — At a walking pace
Allegro — Quickly

NOVEMBER NIGHT

Poem

A. Crapsley

Listen . . .
With faint dry sound,
Like steps of passing ghosts.

The leaves, frost-crisp'd, break from the
trees
And fall.

NOVEMBER

Note/Rote Song

Scandinavian Melody/English Lyrics by J. Wood

Dm(F): d t, l, d m d l,   1 2 sing

This song is written in a **minor key.**

Change the home tone, **lah,** to **doh** and sing it in the major key.

Why do you think the composer chose a **minor key?**

Andante   Dm   Gm   Dm

1. Chil - ly winds from the north bring the cold   and the snow
2. And the dew   on the lawn, that in spring - time had shone

Gm   Dm

As   the year   quick - ly comes   to   its   close.
Like bright dia - monds, turns quick - ly   to   frost.

F   Gm   Dm

Branch-es brown on the wall   by   the old chim-ney tall
With -ered flowers in the yard, stiff, with stems froz - en hard,

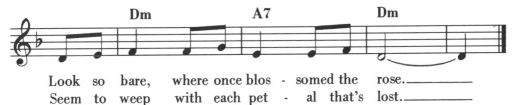

Dm   A7   Dm

Look so bare, where once blos - somed the rose._____
Seem to weep   with each pet - al that's lost._____

31

FINDING DOH WITH SHARPS

When there are **sharps** in the **key signature**, the sharp closest to the notes is **ti**.

Count up one step to **doh'**, or down six steps to **doh**:

    t   d'   t   d

Where is **doh** in each of these examples?

Look at the song "He's Got the Whole World in His Hands."
   Where is **doh**?
   On what note does the melody begin?
   On what note does it end?

HE'S GOT THE WHOLE WORLD

Note/Rote Song

Spiritual

G: d m s___   1 2 3 4 1 2 sing

1. He's got the whole_____ world in His hands,
2. He's got the ti - ny lit - tle ba - by in His hands,

He's got the whole wide__ world in His hands,
He's got the ti - ny lit - tle ba - by in His hands,

He's got the whole_____ world in His hands,
He's got the ti - ny lit - tle ba - by in His hands,

He's got the whole world in His hands.
He's got the whole world in His hands.

3. He's got the wind and the rain, in His hands . . .

4. He's got everybody here, in His hands . . .

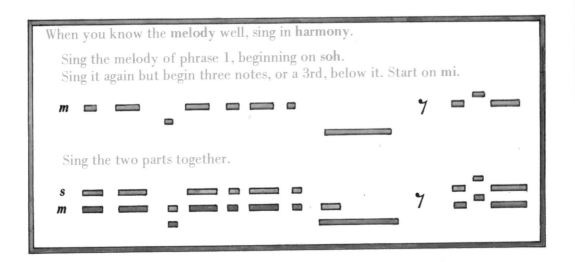

When you know the **melody** well, sing in **harmony**.

Sing the melody of phrase 1, beginning on **soh**.
Sing it again but begin three notes, or a 3rd, below it. Start on **mi**.

Sing the two parts together.

THE STRANGEST DREAM

Rote Song

Ed McCurdy

D: d' s m d m s   1 2 3 1 sing

A Canadian folk singer, Ed McCurdy, wrote this song in 1950.
It expresses people's longing for peace around the world.

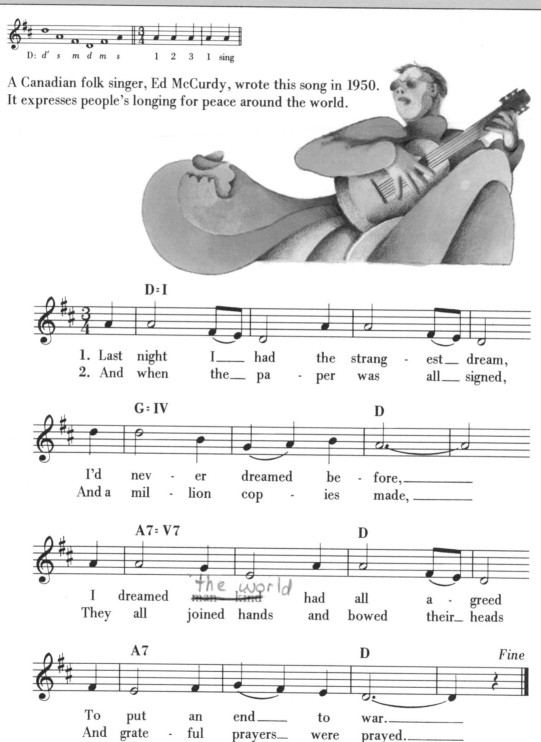

D=I

1. Last night I had the strang - est dream,
2. And when the pa - per was all signed,

G=IV   **D**

I'd nev - er dreamed be - fore,
And a mil - lion cop - ies made,

A7=V7   **D**

I dreamed ~~man - kind~~ *the world* had all a - greed
They all joined hands and bowed their heads

A7   **D**   *Fine*

To put an end to war.
And grate - ful prayers were prayed.

I dreamed I saw a might - y room
And the peo - ple in the streets be - low

And the room was full of men,_____
Were_ danc - ing 'round and 'round,_____

And the pa - per they were sign - ing said
While swords and guns and u - ni - forms

D.C. al Fine

They'd nev - er_____ fight___ a - gain._____
Were scat - tered_ on_____ the ground._____ *(Repeat v. 1)*

This song uses **I (doh)**, **IV (fah)** and **V (soh) chords.**
Why do you think they are named with the numbers **I, IV** and **V**?

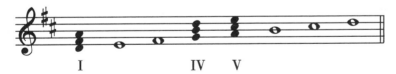

I IV V

The V chord sometimes has a note added to make it sound richer. It is then called a **V7 chord.** Find the V7 chords in the song.

Accompany the song on autoharp or bells. The chord tones are:

A	D	G
F#	B	E
D	G	C#
		A

I = D   IV = G   V7 = A7

SIX-EIGHT TIME

The **time signature** $\frac{6}{8}$ tells us there are six beats in every bar and every eighth note (♪) gets one beat.

The most common patterns in $\frac{6}{8}$ time are:

Find combinations of these patterns in *"Vive l'amour."* When you know the song well, sing it with a feeling of two strong pulses per bar:

VIVE L'AMOUR

Note/Rote Song

Camp Song

G: d m s m d s,   1   2   1   sing

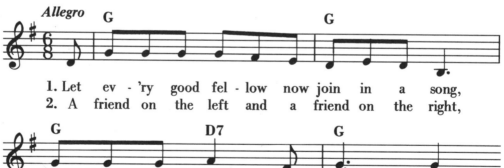

Allegro   G   G

1. Let ev - 'ry good fel - low now join in a song,
2. A friend on the left and a friend on the right,

G   D7   G

Vi - ve la com - pa - gnie. _____

G   G

Suc - cess to each oth - er and pass it a - long,
In love and good fel - low - ship let us u - nite.

G   D7   G

Vi - ve la com - pa - gnie.

36

Chorus

G   C

Vi - ve la, vi - ve la, vi - ve l'a - mour,

D7   G

Vi - ve la, vi - ve la, vi - ve l'a - mour,

Em   Am

Vi - ve l'a - mour,   vi - ve l'a - mour,

D7   G

Vi - ve la com - pa - gnie!_____

Use the I, IV and V7 chords to accompany the song on bells or piano.

THE WRAGGLE-TAGGLE GYPSIES

Note/Rote Song

Scottish Ballad

Dm(F): *d t, l, d m*   1   2   1   sing

A **ballad** is a song that tells a story, usually with many verses. How will you use your voice to tell the story best? Decide how many solos there are. Sing the song using solo and group singing.

	Dm	Gm	Dm
1.	There were three	gyp - sies a - come	to my door,
2.	Then__ she pulled off	her__ silk	fin - ished gown,
3.	It was late last	night when my lord	came__ home,

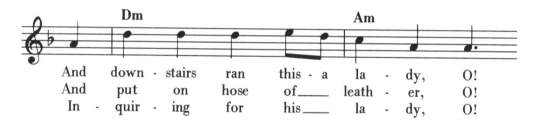

	Dm		Am
And	down - stairs ran	this - a la - dy,	O!
And	put on	hose of__ leath - er,	O!
In -	quir - ing for	his__ la - dy,	O!

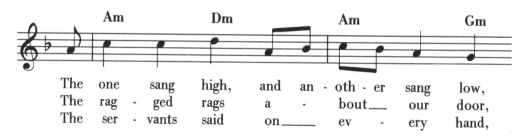

Am	Dm	Am	Gm
The one sang high,	and an - oth - er	sang low,	
The rag - ged rags	a - bout__	our door,	
The ser - vants said	on__ ev -	ery hand,	

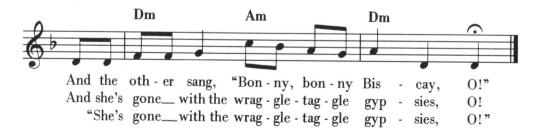

Dm	Am	Dm
And the oth - er sang, "Bon - ny, bon - ny Bis - cay,		O!"
And she's gone__ with the wrag - gle - tag - gle gyp - sies,		O!
"She's gone__ with the wrag - gle - tag - gle gyp - sies,		O!"

4. "Come saddle to me my milk-white steed,
And go and seek my pony, O!
That I may ride and seek my bride,
Who is gone with the wraggle-taggle gypsies, O!"

5. Then he rode high, and he rode low,
He rode through wood and copses too.
Until he came to an open field,
And there he espied his-a lady, O!

6. "What makes you leave your house and your land?
What makes you leave your money, O!
What makes you leave your new-wedded lord,
To go with the wraggle-taggle gypsies, O!"

7. "What care I for my house and my land?
And what care I for my money, O!
What care I for my new-wedded lord?
I'm off with the wraggle-taggle gypsies, O!"

8. "Last night you slept in a goose-feather bed
With the sheet turned down so bravely, O!
But tonight you sleep in a cold, open field,
Along with the wraggle-taggle gypsies, O!"

9. "Oh, what care I for a goose-feather bed
With the sheet turned down so bravely, O!
For tonight I shall sleep in a cold, open field,
Along with the wraggle-taggle gypsies, O!"

Two small groups can perform each of these patterns with the song:

1.	m	r	m
2.	l,	s,	l,
	Bis	- cay -	o

What is a repeated pattern called?

ART DESCRIBES

Sometimes visual artists create a work of art from a small idea, for example, a geometric shape. It is repeated and varied to form the complete work.

Sometimes artists portray an event which suggests an entire story.

What story do you feel the artist had in mind when this painting was created?

Everyone sees art differently.

What art elements in the painting led you
to make your conclusion?

Discuss the reactions of various class members.

MUSIC DESCRIBES

The ballad is a type of song that tells a story. Composers also write **instrumental music** to suit a story they have in mind. An **orchestra** is a large group, or **ensemble**, of musicians which contains all **families of instruments**. Identify the families in the **orchestra**.

Different instruments have distinct **tone colours.** Combining them in different ways creates various effects in music and can suggest action, characters or mood. Orchestral music that represents a story is called **program music.**

LISTENING:

"In the Hall of the Mountain King" from *Peer Gynt Suite*

Edvard Grieg

Peer Gynt is a Norwegian folk character. He is a strong, good-looking boy, but full of mischief. After stealing a bride from her wedding, he is chased up the mountains where he meets a troll princess sunbathing on a rock. They discover that they are both fun-loving rascals and become friends. Peer agrees to follow the troll through the deep dark tunnels of the mountain to meet her father, the king of the trolls.

The music tells the rest of the story. Listen to find out what happens to Peer when he reaches the Hall of the Mountain King. How does the music tell you this has happened?

Listen again. How many times does the composer, Edvard Grieg, use this rhythm to tell the story? Listen carefully. Count only the times it is exactly like this:

Be a musician. Help tell the story.
Silently play the cymbals at the end of the piece.
Whisper the numbers that represent beats. Play only on the
numbers indicated:

1 (2) 3 4 5 (6) 7 8
1 2 3 4 5 6 7 8
1 (2) 3 4 5 (6) 7 8
1 2 3 4 5 6 7 8
1 (2) 3 4 5 (6) 7 8
1 (2) (3) (4) (5) (6) (7) (8)
1 2 3 4 5 6 7 8
1 (2)

VRENELI

Rote Song

Swiss Folk Song

Eb: d′ s m d s, 1 2 3 4 1 2 3 sing

Map the **phrases** in this song as you sing.
**Which phrases go up at the end? Which phrases go down?
Which ones end on the home tone?**

1. "O Vren - e - li, my pret - ty one, Pray tell me where's your home?"
2. "O Vren - e - li, my pret - ty one, Pray tell me where's your heart?"
3. "O Vren - e - li, my pret - ty one, Pray tell me where's your head?"

1. 2.

"My home it is in Switz - er - land, It's made of wood and stone, stone."
"Oh, that," she said, "I gave a - way, Its pain will not de - part, part."
"Oh, that I al - so gave a - way, 'Tis with my heart," she said, said.

Chorus Yo, ho, ho;_____ Yo, ho, ho;_____ Yo, ho,

Yo, ho, ho, tra - la - la - la; Yo, ho, ho, tra - la - la - la; Yo, ho,

1. ho;_____ Yo, ho, ho;_____

ho, tra - la - la - la; Yo, ho, ho, tra - la - la - la;

2. ho,_____ tra - la; Yo, ho, ho.

ho, tra - la - la - la; Yo, ho, ho.

44

SOFIA

Note/Rote Song

Triestine Folk Melody/Lyrics by M. Fishback

A: d m s m d s,   1   2   1   sing

Sometimes notes are altered by adding signs called **accidentals**. **Accidentals** are **sharps ♯**, **flats ♭** or **naturals ♮** that are not in the key signature. Find the **accidentals** in this song.

1. I'm be-witched by a girl named So-fi-a,

With a nose like a full-blown bal-loon.

And her bar-ba-rous teeth are a jag-ged saw

That glint by the light of the moon. What can I do?

What can I do? En-chant-ing So-fi-a, I'm mad a-bout you.

2. All day long and at night she sits watching
On her balcony over the lane.
And with patience she lurks there and waits for me
I tell you she drives me insane.

FRENCH LULLABY

Note/Rote Song

Composer Unknown

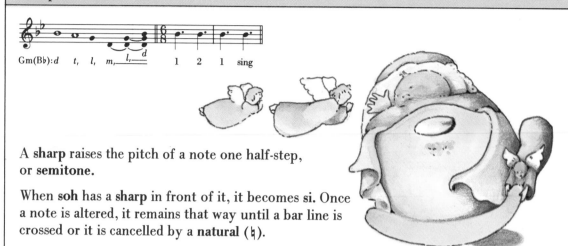

A **sharp** raises the pitch of a note one half-step, or **semitone**.

When **soh** has a **sharp** in front of it, it becomes **si**. Once a note is altered, it remains that way until a bar line is crossed or it is cancelled by a **natural** (♮).

Find the **sharp** notes, or **accidentals**, in this song.

Chorus

Tou-tou-ie lon la, my dear one, Tou-tou-ie__ lon la.____ la.

Loo, _____ Loo. ____

Verse

1. Thy fa - ther is com - ing, Thy moth - er is nigh,
2.   Life will know sor - row and hun - ger and cold.
3. Let God be thy keep - er and Je - su thy guide,

D.C. al Fine

To com - fort her dear one, so hushed be thy cry.
May faith then sus - tain thee un - til thou art old.
With moth - er to com - fort and strength-en be - side.

WINTER

O HANUKAH

Note Song

Jewish Folk Song/Trans. by J. Eisenstein

Dm(F): d t, l, d m d l,   1 2 3 sing

O Ha - nu - kah, O Ha - nu - kah, come light the me - no - rah,

Let's have a par - ty, we'll all dance the ho - ra.

Gath - er round the ta - ble, we'll give you a treat,

Shin - ing tops to play with and pan - cakes to eat;

And while we are play - ing the can - dles are burn - ing_ low.

One for each night, they_ shed a sweet light To re -

1. mind us of days long a - go.   2. mind us of days long a - go.

ENTENDEZ-VOUS LE CARILLON?

Rote Song and Round

French

F: *d   m   s   d'   s*   1   2   sing

Look at the melody of the song before you sing.

Find a passage that moves down by **step.**

How many **skips** can you find?

En - ten-dez-vous   le   ca - ril - lon, di-ri don, don,

don,   di - ri don,   don,   don,   don,   don,   don?

THE BALLAD OF JESUS CHRIST

Note Song

Old French

Dm(F): *d t, l, d m d l,* 1 2 3 sing

The first phrase of this song has six measures. Where is it **repeated**?
Call each of these phrases **A**.

Find the **contrasting** phrase. How many measures does it have?
What will you call it?

1. One in rag - ged robes came a - beg - ging,
2. But my la - dy there at the win - dow,
3. When the beg - gar, hum - bly a - ris - ing,

"Please to give me char - i - ty.
Heard his plea for char - i - ty.
Blessed her for her char - i - ty,

May I have the scraps from your ta - ble
"Do come in, my poor hun - gry fel - low,
Then my la - dy star - ing in won - der

To ap - pease my hun - ger?" quoth he.
Do come in and sup with___ me.
All a - round a ra - diance could see.

Dm	Gm	Dm	A7

"Oh, no," said my lord, "My dogs— I must feed.
And if you are tired and wea - ry,
Je - sus Christ the Lord had bless - ed her:

Dm	A7	Dm

So for you there's noth - ing from me."
We've a bed for you here," said she.
For in - deed the beg - gar was He!

CHRISTMAS CUSTOMS

Christmas customs have come to us from around the world. Many popular ones came from England. The hanging of mistletoe and the use of holly for decoration are among the oldest. In the mid-1800s sending Christmas cards became popular.

Food is an important part of any festival. The boar's head was a popular main dish at least until the time of King Henry VIII. Turkey with dressing is now the most popular meat served for Christmas dinner. The English pudding made with meat, apples, plums, brandy and sugar is also still a favourite.

Carollers often went from door to door, singing carols as entertainment for people in their homes. Sometimes they would be invited in to share Christmas goodies with the family. The songs on the next few pages would be good selections for you to use on an evening of carolling.

These Christmas customs bring joy and cheer in the middle of winter for many Canadians. Other people, here and around the world, celebrate mid-winter festivals in other ways. Find out about other customs from your friends of different backgrounds.

Merrie Christmas

GOD REST YOU MERRY, GENTLEMEN

Rote Song

English

Em(G): d t, l, d m d l, 1 2 1 sing

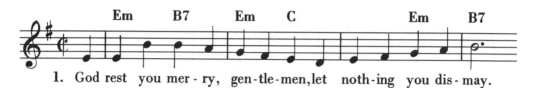

Em   B7   Em   C   Em   B7

1. God rest you mer - ry, gen-tle-men, let noth-ing you dis - may.

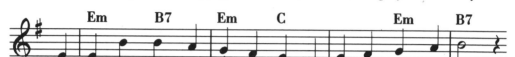

Em   B7   Em   C   Em   B7

Re - mem-ber Christ our Sav - iour was born on Christ-mas day;

Am   G   G   C   D   D7

To save us all from Sa - tan's pow'r when we were gone a - stray.

Chorus

G   B7   Em   D

Oh,___ tid - ings of com - fort and joy, com-fort and joy,

G   B7   Em

Oh,___ tid - ings of com - fort and joy.

2. In Bethlehem in Jewry this blessed Babe was born.
And laid within a manger, upon this blessed morn;
The which His mother Mary did nothing take in scorn.

3. Now to the Lord sing praises, all you within this place.
And with true love and brotherhood each other now embrace;
This holy tide of Christmas all other doth deface.

A SOALIN'

Rote Song

T. Batteast, E. Messetti and P. Stookey

Em(G): d t, l, d m d l,   1   2   1   sing

Listen to the recording. Discover ostinatos that use the notes E, F♯, G and A. Create an accompaniment for this series of songs.

Hey,   ho,   no - bod-y home, Meat nor drink nor mon-ey have I

none.   Yet   shall   we   be   mer   -   ry, —

Coda

Hey,   ho,   no - bod-y home. Hey,   ho,   no - bod-y home.

*Try this as a round.

53

Chorus

d   d   t,   t,   d   l,   d   d   t,   t,   t,   d   l,   l,

Soal, a soal, a soal - cake, Please, good mis-tress, a soal - cake, An

d   d   d   t,   t,   d   d   t,   t,   d   d   d   t,   t,

ap - ple, a pear, a plum, a cher-ry, An - y good thing to

d   d   d   t,   t,   d   d   t,   t,   d   d   l,

make us all mer - ry, One for Pe - ter, two for Paul,

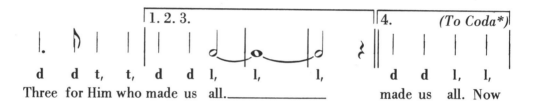

1. 2. 3.   **4.**   *(To Coda*)*

d   d   t,   t,   d   d   l,   l,   l,   d   d   l,   l,

Three for Him who made us all._____ made us all. Now

Verse

1. God bless the mas - ter of this house and the mis - tr - ess al - so,
2. Go down in - to the cel - lar and_ see what you can find,
3. The streets are ver - y dir - ty, my_ shoes are ver - y thin,

And all the lit - tle chil - dren that 'round your ta - ble grow.
If the bar - rels are not emp - ty we hope you will be kind.
I have a lit - tle pock - et to put a pen - ny in.

The cat - tle in your sta - ble, the dog by your front door,
We hope you will be kind with your ap - ples and your ale,
If you hav - en't got a pen - ny a ha' - pen - ny will do,

(To Chorus)

And all that dwells with-in your gates, we wish you ten times more.
For we'll come no more a soal - in' till this__ time next year.
If you have-n't got a ha'-pen-ny then God__ bless__ you.

*Coda

to the Lord sing prais - es, all you with - in this place.

And with true love and broth-er - hood each oth - er now em-brace.

This ho - ly tide of Christ - mas, of beau - ty and of grace,

Oh__ tid - ings of com - fort and joy.

55

CALYPSO CAROL

Rote Song

Richard Graves

F: *d m s m d s,*   1 2 3 4 1 2 sing

Listen to the percussion instruments on the recording. Find the sound of the claves. Practice clapping the claves' rhythm as you sing. Follow the x's on the score.

1. When Jesus Christ____ our Lord was born, ____ The
2. Two thousand years____ have come and gone__ Since the
3. It may not be__ in a stable bare, ____ There

an-gels wel-comed that hap-py morn; The world was wea-ry, the
star of Beth-le-hem bright-ly shone; And now a-gain____ the
won't be wise men and shep-herds there; But when Lord Je-sus is

world was sad,__ So down came Je-sus to make us glad; And
world is torn__ With war and hun-ger and fear and scorn; There's
born a-gain,__ Oh, may it be__ in the hearts of man; And

Last time to Coda

bells____ rang, An-gels____
all the bells__ on earth__ rang, And all the an-gels in
fight-ing while__ the bells__ ring, There's hat-ing while____ the
all the bells__ on earth will ring, And

sang:
Heav-en sang:__ "Peace on earth and good-will__ to-wards men.
an-gels sing;__ Not much peace or good-will__ to-wards men.

56

Peace on earth_ and good-will_____ to-wards men."
Not much peace_ or good-will_____ to-wards men.

Coda

all the an - gels in Heav - en sing,_ For Christ our Lord_ will

real - ly bring Peace on earth and good-will_ to-wards men;

Peace on earth_ and good-will to - wards men._____

Accompany the song.
Take turns playing
these ostinatos:

IN THE TOWN

Rote Song

French Melody

Dm(F): d t, l, d m d l, 1 2 3 1 sing

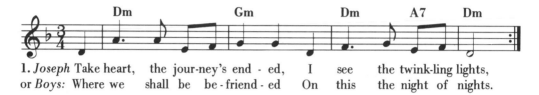

1. *Joseph* Take heart, the jour-ney's end - ed, I see the twink-ling lights,
or *Boys:* Where we shall be be - friend - ed On this the night of nights.

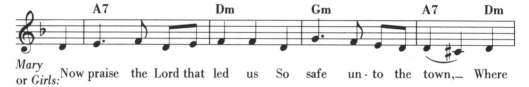

Mary
or *Girls:* Now praise the Lord that led us So safe un - to the town,— Where

men will feed and bed us, And I can lay me down.

h

2. *Joseph:*
And how then shall we praise Him?
Alas my heart is sore
That we no gifts can raise Him
Who are so very poor.

Mary:
We have as much as any
That on the earth do live,
Although we have no penny,
We have ourselves to give.

3. *Joseph:*
Look yonder, wife, look yonder!
An hostelry I see,
Where travellers that wander,
Will very welcome be.

Mary:
The house is tall and stately,
The door stands open thus:
Yet, husband, I fear greatly
That inn is not for us.

4. *Joseph:*
God save you, gentle master!
Your little rooms indeed
With plainest walls of plaster
Tonight will serve our need.

Host:
For lordlings and for ladies
I've lodging and to spare;
For you and yonder maid is
No closet anywhere.

5. *Joseph:*
Take heart, take heart, sweet Mary,
Another inn I spy,
Whose host will not be chary
To let us easy lie.

6. *Joseph:*
God save you, hostess, kindly!
I pray you, house my wife,
Who bears beside me blindly
The burden of her life.

7. *Joseph:*
Good woman, I implore you
Afford my wife a bed.

   Hostess:
Nay, nay, I've nothing for you
Except the cattle-shed.

8. *Joseph:*
Take heart, take heart, sweet Mary,
The cattle are our friends;
Lie down, lie down, sweet Mary,
For here the journey ends.

Mary:
Oh aid me, I am ailing,
My strength is nearly gone;
I feel my limbs are failing,
And yet we must go on.

Hostess:
My guests are rich men's daughters
And sons, I'd have you know!
Seek out the poorer quarters
Where ragged people go.

Mary:
Then gladly in the manger
Our bodies we will house,
Since men tonight are stranger
Than asses are and cows.

Mary:
Now praise the Lord that found me
This shelter in the town,
Where I with friends around me
May lay my burden down.

This song uses only three chords —
the **I**, the **IV** and the **V7 chords.**

  Which beat is **accented** in each bar?
Strum on the **accented beats.**

Find bars in which the chord changes on
the third beat. Add a short, light
strum on these **weak beats.**

HOLIDAY BLESSING

Rote Song

Music and Lyrics by Joyce Elaine Eilers

Eb: d' s m—d   1   2   1   sing

Remember? |1. |2.

Which bars will you leave out the first time you sing? the second?

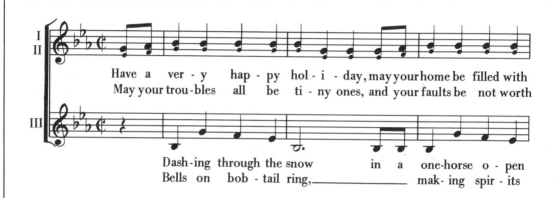

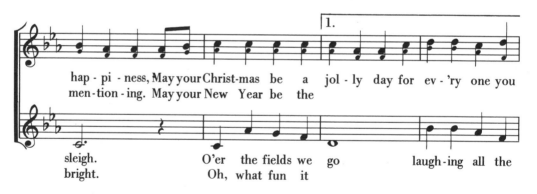

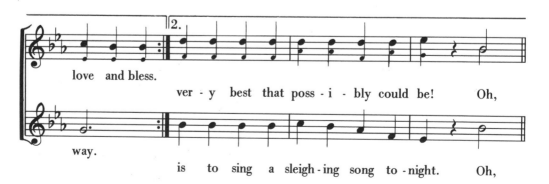

Feel the two beats (𝅘𝅥's) in each bar by conducting:

1
2

strong   weak

61

LITTLE JACK HORNER

Note Song and Round

A.E. Wilshire

F:*d* *m* *s* *m* *d*   1   2   1   sing

Lit-tle Jack Hor-ner sat in a cor-ner eat-ing his Christ-mas

pie.   He   put   in his thumb and he pulled out a plum and he

said,   "Myum,   myum,   myum,   myum! What a good boy!

What a good boy! What a   good boy am I."

JAPANESE CHRISTMAS CAROL

Note Song

Traditional Japanese Melody/Lyrics by Rev. S. Ojima/Trans. by K. Hanson and T. Lee

Ebm(Gb): *d   t,   l,   d   m   d   l,*   1   2   1   sing

Find phrases that show **repetition**.
Repetition gives **unity** to a piece of music.
Find the **contrasting** phrase.
This contrast adds **interest** to the song.

1. Low - ly shep-herds of Ju - de - a, on a win ter's night,
2. Wise men seek - ing Je - sus' man - ger, trav-elled from a - far;
3. Hap - py child-ren sing - ing car - ols to the Ho - ly Boy,

Heard a sound of an - gel voic - es, saw a won-drous light.
Soon their hearts were filled with glad -ness, led there by the star.
Round the world at Christ-mas join us with their songs of joy.

Refrain

Come, child - ren, car - ol mer - ry, *Koo - ree - soo - mah - soo.*

Let us all be ver - y mer - ry, *Koo - ree - soo - mah - soo.*

THE HURON CAROL

Rote Song

French Melody/English Lyrics by J.E. Middleton

1. 'Twas in the moon of win-ter-time, When all the birds had fled,
2. With-in a lodge of bro-ken bark The ten-der Babe was found,

That might-y Git-chi Man-i-tou Sent an-gel choirs in-stead;
A rag-ged robe of rab-bit skin En-wrapped His beau-ty 'round;

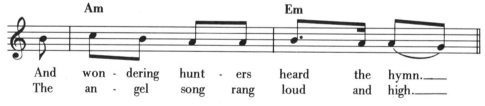

Be - fore their light the stars grew dim,
But as the hunt - er braves drew nigh,

And won - dering hunt - ers heard the hymn.___
The an - gel song rang loud and high.___

Chorus

"Je - sus your King is born, Je - sus is born,

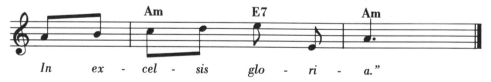

In ex - cel - sis glo - ri - a."

3. The earliest moon of wintertime   The helpless Infant there.
Is not so round and fair   The chiefs from far before Him knelt
As was the ring of glory on   With gifts of fox and beaver pelt.

THIS LAND, CANADA

I am Canada. I stretch thousands of miles from the
Pacific Ocean on the west coast, across mountains,
fields, forests and lakes to the great Atlantic Ocean.
My ten provinces and two territories across this
great land are home to millions of people living here.

You are one of them. How proud you must feel
that you are native to this land; or that your mother
and father chose to live in Canada. Perhaps some of
you have lived in a province other than the one you
live in now; perhaps in another country.

Jo and Rudy Toth

CANADA BLUES

American Folk Blues/Canadian Version by P. Brooks

G:*d m s m d*   1 2 3 sing

This song in **blues style** takes us on a musical trip across Canada. What musical elements give it a "blue" feeling?

Snap your fingers on the x 's.

1. Start - ed in   the east,___   it was   fine,   I
2. Cloud - y   in   Que-bec,___   looked like   rain,   I

trav - elled all   o - ver the___ Mar - i - times.   In Hal - i -
spent all   my   mon - ey on the sub - way   train.   In Mon - tre -

fax,___   in Hal - i -
al,___   in Mon - tre -

fax,___   And in   Grand   Falls,___ you
al,___   And in   To - ron - to, you

real - ly got - ta know your   way!_____
                                (know your   way!)

66

3. Moved farther west, saw the sun
Shining all over Saskatchewan.
In Saskatoon, in Maple Creek
And in Prince Albert, you really gotta know your way!

4. Farther west again, it was cold,
But when I saw the mountains, now, I was sold.
In Calgary, in Lake Louise,
And in Peace River, you really gotta know your way!

5. Right to the coast, ocean blue,
Boy, how my love of the Pacific grew,
In Campbell River, in Burnaby,
And in Nanaimo, you really gotta know your way!

MACKENZIE RIVER

Note/Rote Song

R. Hyslop and D. Halhed

D: d' s m d   1 2 3 4 1 2 sing

1. Through Can - a - da's north - west fron - tier,   from Great Slave Lake at the
2. Through most of the year the   riv - er's capped with ice and a blan - ket of

south, Our long - est riv - er, Mac-ken - zie, flows north to its del - ta
snow. But in the months when the sun shines, Mac - ken - zie's wa - ters

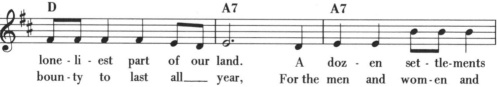

mouth.   Twelve hun - dred miles   it twists   its course through the
flow.   The river's a - live with barges and tugs stacked with

lone - li - est part of our land.   A doz - en set - tle-ments
boun - ty to last all___ year,   For the men and wom-en and

mark its course, through scen-er - y,   awe - some and grand.
chil - dren of our Can - a - da's north-west fron - tier.

Chorus

Sing your sum - mer song,   Mac - ken - zie Riv - er,

Sing of the joy you give, Of your barg-es and car-go you de-

liv - er, So the folks down riv - er can live.

Find the four-bar phrases in this song.
Which sound **unfinished**? Which sound **finished**?
On what note do the finished phrases come to rest?

LEARN TO PLAY THE UKULELE

This is a standard ukulele:

This triangular version
was developed by
the Canadian ukulele expert,
Chalmers Doane.

Once you're seated in correct
playing position,

strum the strings in a downward
motion with the fingernail of your
right-hand index finger. (Use your
left thumb behind the fretboard to
keep the instrument steady.)

Pluck each string.
What do you notice
about the pitches?

The fingers of your
left hand are numbered:

1st finger
2nd finger
3rd finger
4th finger

Try playing chords to accompany your singing.

Chord symbols tell you which string to press and which fingers to use.

G

This one tells you to press the second string with your 1st finger and the fourth string with your 2nd finger:

What do these chord symbols tell you to do?

Try strumming these two chords:
Strum the chord when its name appears and on each stroke that follows.

G / / / **D7** / / /

Now strum as you sing this song:

G / / / / / / /

There was an old man called Michael Finnigin,

D7 / / / / / / /

He grew whiskers on his chinigin.

Here are two new chords:

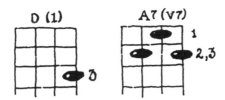

When fingering A7, push your wrist away from you to let your 3rd finger fit on the first string.

Use the **G**, **D**, and **A7** chords to accompany "Mackenzie River."
Strum on every beat and accent beats one and three. You can accompany the next song with the same chords.
Accent beat one only.

SQUID-JIGGIN' GROUND

Rote Song

A.R. Scammell

D: d' s m d m s   1 2 3 1 sing

Arthur Scammell grew up in one of the fishing villages along the north shore of New-foundland. In this song he tells of one way to make a living from the sea — fishing, or "jigging", for squid. The squid is an octopus-like mollusc with ten tentacles. It is used for bait and as food.

1. Oh! This is the place where the fish - er - men gath - er,
2. Some are work - ing their jig - gers while oth - ers are yarn - in',

In oil - skins and boots and Cape - Anns bat - tened down.
There's some stand - in' up and there's more ly - in' down.

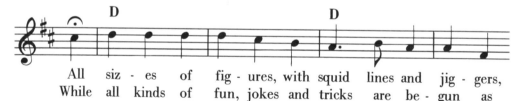

All siz - es of fig - ures, with squid lines and jig - gers,
While all kinds of fun, jokes and tricks are be - gun as

They con - gre - gate here on the squid - jig - gin' ground.
They wait for the squid on the squid - jig - gin' ground.

3. There's poor Uncle Billy, his whiskers are spattered
With spots of the squid juice that's flyin' around;
One poor little b'y got it right in the eye,
But they don't give a darn on the squid-jiggin' ground.

4. Now if ever you feel inclined to go squiddin'
Leave your white shirts and collars behind in the town.
And if you get cranky without yer silk hanky,
You'd better steer clear of the squid-jiggin' ground.

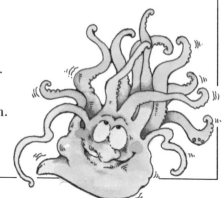

FORTY BELOW

Note/Rote Song

Canadian Folk Song

G: *d m s m d s,*   1 2 3 4 1 2 sing

This version of a well-known Canadian folk melody comes from Winnipeg, probably from the 1920s. The first verse refers to the immigrants who settled Manitoba in the 1880s. Because of the high cost of running farms and the bad weather conditions, many settlers gave up and returned east.

1. Oh, my grand - pa came west in the eight - ies,   To the prai - ries where
Chorus: Oh, it's for - ty be - low in the win - ter,   And it's twen - ty be -

grain grows likes grass.   But the Wheat Board and freight rates got
low in the fall;   And it ris - es to zer - o in

grand - pa,   And so grand - pa went east sec - ond class.
spring - time,   And we don't have no sum - mer at all.

2. It was raining and hailing this morning
On the corner of Portage and Main.
Now it's noon and the basements are flooded,
And the duststorms are starting again.

3. Come and pay for my fare if you love me,
And I'll hasten to bid you adieu;
And farewell to your Red River Valley,
And its natives all shivering and blue.

This song uses three chords. You know the I and V7 chords on the ukulele.

Now try the C major chord: Press the first and second strings with your 1st finger.

Accompany the song.

MON PAYS

Rote Song

Gilles Vigneault

C: d' s m d m s d' t d'   1 2 3 1 sing

In this song, popular singer Gilles Vigneault compares his feelings of
emptiness, confusion, sadness and loneliness to the snowy coldness
and storms of the Canadian winter.

Gilles Vigneault has written many poems and songs
about the people and life in his
native Quebec.

He won first prize at the International Song Festival in 1965 with
this song.

1. Mon pa-ys, ce n'est pas un pa-ys, c'est l'hi-ver;
2. Mon pa-ys, ce n'est pas un pa-ys, c'est l'hi-ver;
3. Mon pa-ys, ce n'est pas un pa-ys, c'est l'en-vers

Mon jar-din, ce n'est pas un jar-din, c'est la plaine;
Mon re-frain, ce n'est pas un re-frain, c'est ra-fale;
D'un pa-ys qui n'é-tait ni pa-ys ni pa-trie.

Mon che-min, ce n'est pas un che-min, c'est la neige; Mon pa-
Ma mai-son, ce n'est pas ma mai-son, c'est froi-dure; Mon pa-
Ma chan-son, ce n'est pas ma chan-son, c'est ma vie; C'est pour

ys, ce n'est pas un pa-ys, c'est l'hi-ver.
ys, ce n'est pas un pa-ys, c'est l'hi-ver.
toi que je veux pos-sé-der mes hi - vers.____

HOLY FAMILY SCHOOL

A PLACE TO STAND

Rote Song

Music by D. Claman/Lyrics by R. Morris

Give us a place to stand_____ and a place to grow,_____

_____ And call this land_____ On - tar - i - o._____

1. A place to live_____ for you and me_____
2. From west - ern hills_____ to north - ern shore_____

_____ With hopes as high_____ as the tall - est tree._____
_____ To Niag - 'ra Falls_____ where the wa - ters roar._____

Give us a land of lakes_____ and a land of snow,_____
Give us a land of peace_____ where the free winds blow,_____

_____ And we will build_____ On - tar - i - o._____

_____ A place to stand, a place to grow, On -

tar - i - ar - i - ar - i - o._____ _____

77

DREAMS

Langston Hughes

Poem

Hold fast to dreams
For if dreams die
Life is a broken-winged bird
That cannot fly.

Hold fast to dreams
For when dreams go
Life is a barren field
Frozen with snow.

CAPE BRETON DREAM

Note/Rote Song

D. Ryan and B. Gough

G: *d m s m d*   1 2 3 1 sing

Cape Breton is located at the northern end of Nova Scotia. Among the early settlers were many immigrants from Scotland. They brought with them the Scottish names of their homeland.

Find the Scottish place names mentioned in the song.
Locate them on a map of Nova Scotia.

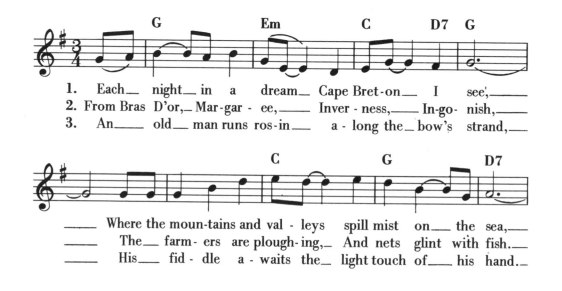

1. Each__ night__ in a   dream__ Cape Bret-on__ I   see,_____
2. From Bras D'or,__ Mar-gar - ee,_____ Inver - ness,_____ In-go- nish,_____
3. An_____ old__ man runs ros-in__ a - long the__ bow's   strand,__

_____ Where the moun-tains and val - leys   spill mist   on__ the sea,____
_____ The__ farm- ers are plough-ing,_ And nets glint with fish.__
_____ His__ fid - dle a - waits the_ light touch of____ his hand._

And mu - sic is call - ing __ through sun - light __ its song __
The kit - chens are smell - ing __ of fresh home - made bread, __
The sun goes be - hind __ the moun - tains __ to leave, __

While the farm - er is wak - ing __ the sky up __ for dawn.
And __ chil - dren are play - ing __ a - long the __ cape head.
And __ bag - pipes are wait - ing __ till night - time __ to breathe.

Chorus

Oh, it's sweet as __ the heath - er __ and rough as __ red wine,

__ Where the mu - sic runs fid - dles __ and pipes through my spine. __

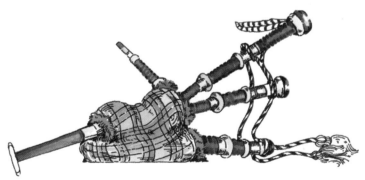

Imitate the drone of the Scottish bagpipes by playing these notes on the piano:

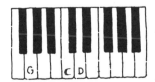

Brumm

Notice this part is written in the **bass clef.** Someone could play G an octave lower to give a richer sound.

SASKATCHEWAN BLUES

Rote Song

Alison Pirot

G: d m s m mah d   1 2 3 4 sing

Here is another Canadian song written in **blues style**. Saskatchewan is the middle prairie province of our Canadian West. Some people complain of the cold winter weather — as this song describes!

Chorus

Gm — Sas-kat - che-wan, go on, go on! A — Gm — Sas-kat - che-wan,

D — go on home. Gm — Sas-kat - che-wan, go on, A — go on!

Gm — So cold in the win - ter, oh, D7 — I wan - na go Gm — home.

Verse

Gm — 1. So cold in the win - ter that I froze my D — nose.

Gm — So cold in the win - ter that I lost all my D — toes.

Gm — Winds just a - how - lin' and the snow's just Cm — a - blow-in',

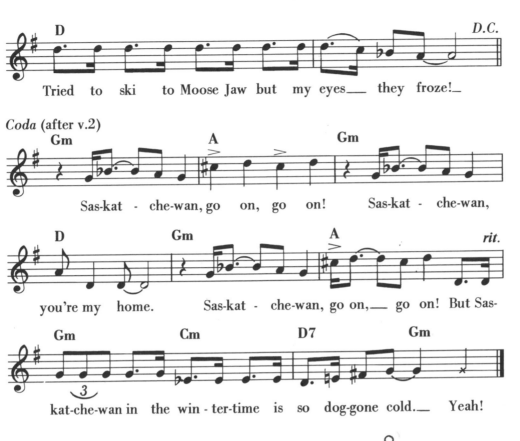

Tried to ski to Moose Jaw but my eyes___ they froze!___

Coda (after v.2)

Gm | **A** | **Gm**

Sas-kat - che-wan, go on, go on! Sas-kat - che-wan,

D | **Gm** | **A** | *rit.*

you're my home. Sas-kat - che-wan, go on,___ go on! But Sas-

Gm | **Cm** | **D7** | **Gm**

kat-che-wan in the win - ter-time is so dog-gone cold.___ Yeah!

2. Lots of bright, warm sunshine
and the bluest skies.
Lots of space for movin' out
to watch the sun rise.
Wind, lightin', thunder
and the sweet smell of grain,
Long days and northern lights,
oh, how the time flies!

81

LABRADOR

Note/Rote Song

Traditional Folk Melody/Lyrics by M. Webb

F: d m s m   1   2   1   sing

Labrador is one section of Canada that is not densely populated. Men who have gone to work in the mines may have felt they were going to the top of the world! It is likely they sang happy songs like this one to build up their courage.

In march style

1. We've formed a band, and our trip's all planned, We'll jour-ney a - far to the
2. A trek we'll make up to far Knob Lake, We'll work in the wilds for___

prom - ised land; For i - ron ore is rich in store, At the
Can-a - da's sake; We'll pi - o - neer this new fron - tier, Like our

Chorus

top of the world in Lab - ra - dor. Then ho, lads, ho, let's
fore - fa-thers bold, with-out a fear.

to Un - ga - va go; There is hem - a - tite in the

north, all right, At the top of the world in Lab - ra - dor.

WINTER NIGHT

Note Song

Scandinavian Melody/Lyrics by C. Winter

Em (G): *d t, l, d m*   1 2 3 sing

Bleak   and   sil - vered   is   the   night, Chill

dia - monds on   the ground   are   ly -   ing.

Up   a - gainst   the   fro - zen   sky,   An
Does   the   wind   call   to   the   trees,   Or

owl   cuts thro' the harsh   air,   cry -   ing.
is   it   just   the   cold   moon   sigh -   ing?

SNOW
I could eat it!
This snow that falls
so softly, so softly.

Issa

WALLY AHCHA

Rote Song

Camp Song

Wal - ly ah - cha, Wal - ly ah - cha,

Doo - dle-ee - doo,— Doo - dle-ee - doo.—

Wal - ly ah - cha, Wal - ly ah - cha, Doo - dle-ee - doo,—

Doo -dle-ee - doo. It's the sim - pl - est thing, there's noth-in' much to_ it.__

All you got -ta do is doo-dle-ee-doo_ it.__ I like the rest but the

part I like best_ goes: Doo-dle-ee - doo - dle-ee-doo. Doo!

84

WADDALY AHCHA

Rote Song

Camp Song

Eb: *d m s m d m* | 1 2 3 sing

Listen to the recording. What song does this remind you of?
Find **variations** in lyrics; in rhythm; in melody.

Wad-dal-ly ah-cha, Wad-dal-ly ah-cha, Doo-dle-ee-doo,

Doo-dle-ee-doo.— Wad-dal-ly ah-cha, Wad-dal-ly ah-cha,

Doo-dle-ee-doo, Doo-dle-ee-doo. It's the sim-pl-est thing, there's

no-thin' much to— it.— All you got-ta do is doo-dle-ee-doo it.—

1. I like the rest but the part I like best it goes: Doo-dle-ee-doo-dle-ee-

2. doo. Doo-dle-ee-doo-dle-ee-doo. Doo!

3 times

Vary the actions you did for "Wally Ahcha."

85

VALENTINE SWING

Rote Song

Music by B. Strachan/Lyrics by B. Strachan and M. Trotter

D: d' s m d   1 2 3 4 1 2 sing

1. Well, I wrote a card on Val - en-tine's Day,—
2. Well, I carved your name on the side of a tree,—

Did - n't sign it, that's__ the way.__
Hopin' you'd know that it was by me.__

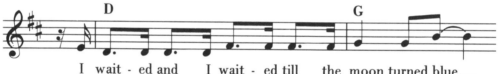

I wait - ed and I wait - ed till the moon turned blue,—
I wait - ed and I wait - ed till I turned blue too,—

But I did - n't get a Val - en - tine from you.—
But I did - n't get a Val - en - tine from you. Oh, yeah!
(Spoken)

IT'S A SMALL WORLD

Music is a universal language.
People in all countries of the world sing
to express their feelings of happiness, sadness, pride or fear.
Songs can also tell of the history and everyday life of a culture.
When people move from one place to another, they carry the heritage
and culture of their homeland with them.

IT'S A SMALL WORLD

Rote Song

Richard M. Sherman and Robert B. Sherman

A: *d m s m d s, m,*   1   2   sing

What does the phrase "It's a small world" mean to you?
Is your idea the same or different from the one expressed in the song?

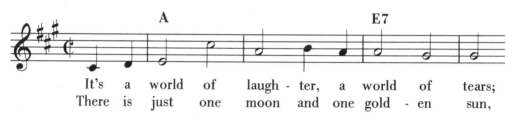

It's   a   world   of   laugh - ter,   a   world   of   tears;
There   is   just   one   moon   and   one   gold - en   sun,

It's   a   world   of   hopes   and   a   world   of   fears.
And   a   smile   means   friend - ship   to   ev - 'ry - one.

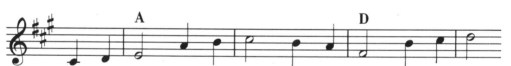

There's so   much   that   we   share   that   it's   time   we're a - ware,
Though the moun - tains di - vide   and the   o - ceans are wide,

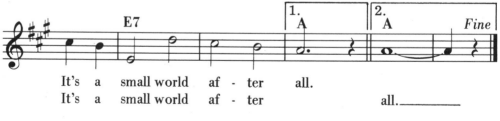

It's   a   small world   af - ter   all.
It's   a   small world   af - ter   all.____

It's   a   small   world   af - ter   all,

E7   A

It's   a   small world   af - ter all,

A   D

It's   a   small world   af - ter all,

E7   A   D.C. al Fine

It's   a small,   small   world._____

Map the melody as you sing.

Find musical ideas that are **repeated.**
Find ideas that show **contrast.**

THE PURPLE BAMBOO

Note Song

Chinese Folk Song

C: *d' s m d m s*   1 2 1 sing

Many Chinese melodies are based on the pentatonic scale.

How many notes are in the scale? Name them.

1. See   I   bring to you pur - ple bam - boo shoot.
2. You must try and grow like the bam - boo tall,

Now 'twill make a love - ly   flute;
Then those part - ing lips   so   small,

But those lips so small   can - not play at all
Soon will play the flute,   made from bam - boo shoot;

On   a   love - ly   gold - en___ flute.
Sil - v'ry tunes will gen - tly___ fall.

Chorus

Ee - tee___ ee,   soon will come the hap - py

1. day.
2. day. My son the flute will play.

Music of different cultures often has a unique sound — sometimes because of the instruments that are used. Some Chinese musical instruments are pictured below.

To what family of instruments do you think each belongs? Why?

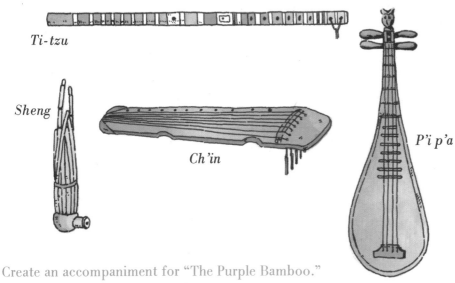

Ti-tzu

Sheng

Ch'in

P'i p'a

Create an accompaniment for "The Purple Bamboo."

Someone could imitate the sound of the flute by playing the melody on a recorder.

Imitate a stringed instrument like the *ch'in*. Press the C major bar of the autoharp. Gently pluck the strings in the upper octave on beat 1 of every bar.

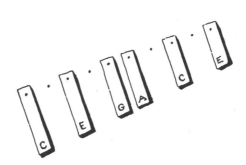

Play these patterns on pitched percussion instruments:

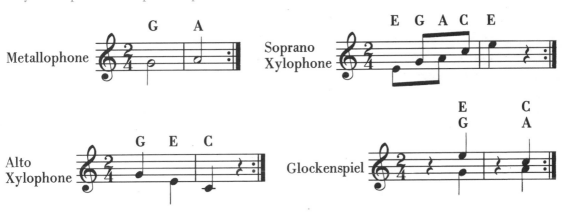

Metallophone

Soprano Xylophone

Alto Xylophone

Glockenspiel

A JAPANESE HAIKU

Buson/Arr. by Nancy Telfer

Poem

Now the moon goes down . . .
slow through the forest, shadows
drift and disappear.

A   Create a melody for the words. Use **d′-l s-m r d.**

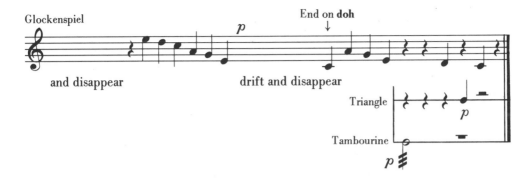

Glockenspiel

p

End on **doh**

and disappear   drift and disappear

Triangle

p

Tambourine

p

B Spoken Part

1) First say the whole poem together.

2) Then create a "word salad." Use these phrases:

Now the moon   drift
    through the forest   slow
and disappear   goes down
        shadows

Choose seven soloists to say these phrases slowly.
The conductor points to each soloist (in any order at all!) and
may point to any or all soloists more than once. The words will
sound all mixed up like a tossed salad (i.e. shadows, slow, now the moon).
Try whispering some phrases.

A Repeat A from the beginning.

CHUNDARI

Rote Song

East Indian Folk Song

G: *d m s m d t, l, s, d t,* 1 2 3 sing

The long silk scarf, or *chundari*, worn by Indian women serves many purposes. In this song, a young man, arriving home much too late, uses a beautiful new *chundari* as a peace offering to his wife. By skillfully holding the *chundari* she is wearing, his wife hides her face from him, yet is able to see him, giving her the advantage in the argument.

Boy: A - tee day-koh nee zha-ra soh, a - tee day-koh nee.
Girl: A - ya kyon neen hoh tay bay-ga a - ya kyon neen hoh.

A - tee day-koh nee zha-ra soh a - tee day-koh nee may lah-yah,
A - ya kyon neen hoh tay bay-ga a - ya kohn neen hoh mayn joh-ha,

Joh - da - da- ree choon da ree tay a - tee day-koh nee.
Ba - tah-tah-ree kahl___ say tay a - ya kyon neen hoh.

Coda

Together: A - tee day-koh nee zha-ra soh, a - tee day-koh nee.

DANCE THE ORO

Rote Song

Macedonian Folk Song/Lyrics by B. Kovacs

B: *d m s m d*   1 2 3 4 5 6 sing

Music and dance are an important part of every culture. This **dance song** is for a circle dance, or *oro*, and comes from the ancient country of Macedonia. Like most dance songs of that area, it uses rhythm patterns combining beat groupings of three and two — making a meter of seven.

Before learning the song, practice this pattern:

1. Cir - cling and sway-ing danc-ers   all___   in   a   row,_____
2. By   the peace-ful Var - dar Riv - er, flow - ing to   the   sea,_____
3. In   the land of songs and danc - es, sun - shine and love._____

Cir - cling and sway-ing danc-ers, join the *o* - ro._____
All___ peo - ple cel - e - brate a land___ that is free._____
Peace and broth-er - hood en-twine as praise to God_ a - bove._____

Chorus

Sing of love,___ sing of hope,___ sing of lib - er - ty.   Oh,_____

In   the land of Ma - ce - do - nia peo - ple shall be   free._____

MINKA

Rote Song

Russian Folk Melody/English Lyrics by W.S. Haynie

Am(C): *d' t l d' m' d' l*   1 2 1 sing

The **minor scale** is often used for melodies that are slow and sad in mood. Though the words in this song tell of someone missing a loved one, the minor tune has a lively, playful quality.

Allegro

1. Min-ka, Min-ka, when I leave thee, How my sad heart al-ways grieves me.

When I'm gone I long to be with Min-ka, Min-ka mine.

When I see the full moon shin-ing, Then I will for thee be pin-ing,

Min-ka, Min-ka, fair-est maid-en, Min-ka, Min-ka mine.

2. When I hear sweet music playing,
Ev'ry note to me is saying,
Minka, Minka, fairest maiden, Minka, Minka mine.
When the winter snow is falling,
I must go, for love is calling,
Calling me to be with Minka, fairest Minka mine.

Listen to the recording for the sound of the *balalaika,* a Russian string instrument. Play the chords of the song on the high strings of the autoharp to imitate the *balalaika.*

WHERE?

Note Song

Ukrainian Folk Song/English Lyrics by M. Diakowsky and D. Sunderland

Em (G): *d t, l, d m d l,*   1   2   1   sing

Many Ukrainian and Russian folk songs have both **major** and **minor** sections.
Which phrases are **minor**? Find a **major** phrase.

1. Where have   all   the birds   gone? Where are   all   the flowers
2. Where have col-oured leaves flown, Where green grass-es   tall,

That gave   so   much beau - ty   to   the   sum - mer hours?
Wav - ing   in   cool breez - es,   whisp-'ring   aut-umn's call?

Chorus

Chased a - way by win - ter,   by   the   ice   and snow.

They'll be   back   in spring - time   when the warm winds blow.

Compare this song
with "Minka."
Discuss **melody**,
rhythm and **form**.

LINSTEAD MARKET

Rote Song

Jamaican Calypso

D: *d′ s m d m s*   1   2   1   sing

Look at the picture. What tells you it's about another country? Listen to the music.
What tells you it's from the Caribbean?

1. Car - ry me ac - kee, go to Lin - stead Mar - ket;
2. Ev - er - y - bod - y come - a Lin - stead Mar - ket;
3. Make__ me call__ it loud - er, "Ac - kee! Ac - kee!

Not a__ quat - ty worth sell.   Car - ry me ac - kee, go to
Not a__ quat - ty worth sell.   Ev - er - y - bod - y come - a
Red and__ pret - ty dem tan.   La - dy, come buy your Sun - day

|G| |D| |A7| | | | |D| |A7|

Lin - stead Mar - ket; Not a___ quat - ty worth sell.   Oh,
fill   up,   fill   up;   Not a___ quat - ty worth sell.   Oh,
morn - ing break - fast; Rice and___ ac - kee nyam gran'."   Oh,

Refrain D   A7   D

No!   Not   a   mite,   not   a   bite,

A7   D   A7   D

what a___ Sat - ur-day night.   Oh,   No!   Not a

A7   D   A7   D

mite, not a bite,   what a___ Sat - ur-day night.

"Linstead Market" is a **calypso**. Calypso songs have strong **syncopated**, or off-beat rhythms and words that are often made up, or **improvised**.

Try improvising rhythms to accompany your singing. Use some of the instruments of the Caribbean shown in the illustration.

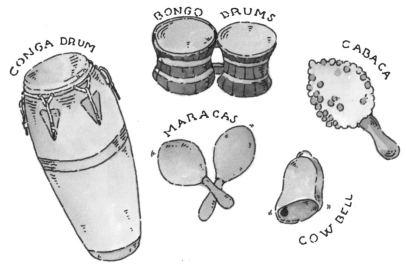

99

MACARONI

Note/Rote Song

Neapolitan Folk Song/English Lyrics Adapted

Em (G):   *d*   *t,*   *l,*   *d*   *m*   1   2   sing

People in Southern Italy once believed the bite of the tarantula spider would make you dance wildly. This is probably how the *tarantella,* a rapid folk dance, got its name. According to legend, it was supposed to cure the spider's bite. What do you think *tempo di tarantella* means?

Tempo di tarantella

Boys

1. I'm   so   poor, hear what I'm say - in', I've   no
2. I   would like   to   be   a   sol - dier In   the
3. My lieu - ten - ant, oh,   so   ar - dent, Changed his

Girls

bed   nor place   to   stay   in. You'd best sell your shirt   for
ar - my, like   I   told   ya. Push the can - non, pull   the
place with his   own ser - geant. Sold his rank   to   get   your

Together

mon - ey, Fat - ten you up   with mac - a - ro - ni. *Ven - de -*
po - ny, Still buy   a dish   of mac - a - ro - ni. *Ven - de -*
mon - ey; Now he will eat   your mac - a - ro - ni. *Ven - de -*

rei   i miei cal - zo - ni, Per un sol plat-to di mac-che-ro - ni.

100

I WENT TO THE MARKET

Rote Song

Canadian

F: *d m s m d s,*   1   2   1   sing

1. I went to the mar-ket *mon p'tit pa - nier sous mon bras.*
2. She said, "What 'ave you got *dans ce beau p'tit pa - nier là?"*

I went to the mar-ket *mon p'tit pa - nier sous mon bras.*
She said, "What 'ave you got *dans ce beau p'tit pa - nier là?"*

The first girl I met was *la fille d'un a - vo - cat.___*
"I've got some ap - ples___ *n'en ach - 'ter - iez - vous pas?"___*

Chorus

"I love you, *vous m'en - ten - dez guè - re,*

I love you, *vous m'en-ten-dez pas." vous m'en-ten-dez pas."*

3. "Oh! Give me two dozen, *pis l'bonhomm' te paiera ça."*
I gave her two dozen, *mais l'bonhomm' y payait pas.*

4. I gave her two dozen, *mais l'bonhomm' y payait pas,*
Such is the business *avec la fille d'un avocat.*

101

THE HARMONIC MINOR SCALE

Look at this scale. Find the **altered note**.
What will you call it?

What is the **home tone**? Sing the scale from the staff
using hand signs. Show si like this:

This is the **harmonic minor scale.**
How is it different from the **natural minor**?

AH, POOR BIRD

Note Song and Round

Traditional

Dm(F):   *d   t,   l,   d   m   d   l,*   1   2   3   sing

Collect and write the notes of this song on the staff.
Order them from low to high. What scale is used?
How do you know? What note is missing?

Ah, poor bird, take thy flight, far a-bove the sor - rows of this sad night.

THE BIRCH TREE

Note/Rote Song

Russian Folk Song

Gm(Bb): *d t, l, d m*   1 2 1   sing

Tschaikovsky, a famous Russian composer of the
nineteenth century, used this folk song melody as a theme
in his Fourth Symphony.

Andante

Gm ... **D7** **Gm** **D7** **Gm**

Vo - po - lay ber - io - za sta - ya - la,
Sil - ver birch a - lone in the mead - ow,

Gm **D7** **Gm** **D7** **Gm**

Vo - po - lay ku - dria - va - ya sta - ya - la,
Stand-ing all a - lone___ in the mead - ow,

D7 **D7** **Gm** **D7** **Gm**

lu - lee, lu - lee, sta - ya - la,
Soon a shepherd boy comes stroll - ing,

D7 **D7** **Gm** **D7** **Gm**

lu - lee, lu - lee, sta - ya - la.
With his sheep and goats left stroll - ing.

THE KEYBOARD FAMILY

Keyboard instruments have changed over the years.
Which of these do you think is the oldest?
Which do you think is the most modern?

What other keyboard
instruments do you
know?
Visit a library to find
out about other
members of this family,
old and new.

WIND SONG

Lillian Moore

Poem

When the wind blows
the quiet things speak.
Some whisper, some clang,
some creak.

Grasses swish.
Treetops sigh.
Flags slap
and snap at the sky.
Wires on poles
whistle and hum.
Ashcans roll.
Windows drum.

When the wind goes —
suddenly
then,
the quiet things
are quiet again.

Use **keyboard sounds** to accompany this poem.

Try — high and low sounds
   — single notes and note clusters
   — pedals and strings

Use **dynamics!**

HAND ME DOWN MY SILVER TRUMPET

Note/Rote Song

Spiritual

F: d m s d' s   1 2 3 4 1 2 sing

For centuries, in many parts of America, black people were forced into slavery. Many slaves helped pass the time as they worked by singing songs. These work songs were called **spirituals** because they often reflected the blacks' deep faith in God. They were often in **call and response** form. One person would sing the lead, or call, and the group would answer. Everyone would sing the chorus.

Call

1. Well, I've nev-er been to Heav'n, but I've— been told,—
2. If re-li-gion were a thing that mon-ey could buy,—
3. Well now, if you want a silver trumpet just— like me,—

Response   *Call*

Hand me down my sil-ver trum-pet, Ga-bri-el. The
The
You'd

gates are made of pearl and the streets are made of gold,
rich— would— live and the poor— would— die,
bet-ter learn to play it in— plen-ty of— time,

106

THE SYNCOPATED CLOCK

Rote Song

Leroy Anderson/Lyrics by Mitchell Parish

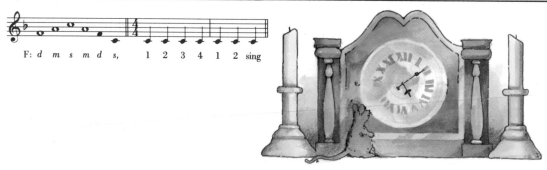

F: d m s m d s, 1 2 3 4 1 2 sing

1. There was a man like you and me,___ as
He had a clock that worked all right,___ it
2. The ex-perts came to hear and see,___ but
But soon the fick-le hu-man race___ will

sim-ple as a man could ev-er be; And he was hap-py
worked all right but not ex-act-ly quite; In-stead of go-ing
none of them could solve the mys-ter-y. They called Pro-fes-sor
find an-oth-er freak to take its place, And one fine day the

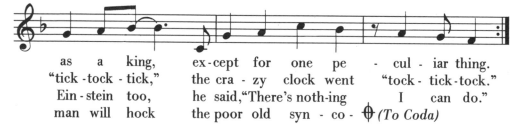

as a king, ex-cept for one pe - cul-iar thing.
"tick-tock-tick," the cra-zy clock went "tock-tick-tock."
Ein-stein too, he said,"There's noth-ing I can do."
man will hock the poor old syn-co- $\oplus$ *(To Coda)*

The poor old man just raved and raved be-cause no-bod-y could

say, Why his sil-ly clock be-haved that

hick- o - ry dick - o - ry way.　　But now a fa - mous

man is he,—— he owns a pub - lic cu - ri - os - i - ty, From

far and wide the peo-ple flock to hear the syn-co - pat - ed clock.

Tick- a -tock, tick - a-tock, tick - a-tock, tick - a-tock, There's a
Ting- a - ling, ting - a-ling, ting - a - ling, ting - a-ling, There's a

zing in the swing of that clock.　Tock - a - tick, tock - a-tick, Tock - a -
zong in the bong of that ring.　Ling - a - ting, ling - a-ting, Ling - a -

1.

tick, tock- a-tick, Don't you think it's a mar - vel-lous trick?
ting, ling - a-ting, Don't you

2.　　　　　　　　　　　　　　　　　　　　　　　　　*D.C.*

think it's a won - der-ful thing?

Coda

Solo

pat　　ed　　clock. Tick-a-tick-tock-tick-tock-tick-tock-tick. Tick! Tock!

CREATE VARIATIONS IN ART

Study these examples of visual art. The subject is the same in both of them. How has the subject been **varied**?

Choose a subject — a scene or an object — you could paint. Discuss, as a class, ways in which you could vary your paintings. Consider elements you work with — colour, texture, pattern, etc. When you have done one or two "variations on your theme," share the results with your classmates.

LISTENING:

"Ah, vous dirai-je, maman"

Wolfgang Mozart

Sometimes composers create a whole composition from one line of melody. A **theme** is repeated many times. Each time, it is changed to create a different effect. This type of musical composition is called **"theme and variations."**

The **theme** of this piece is a well-known children's tune that was written by the famous composer Mozart. Listen to the theme and name it. On what instrument is it played?

Now listen to three **variations** on the theme. As you listen to each one, make a class list of ways the rhythm and melody have been altered, or varied. Use the word pairs below to help you.

Listen to the same theme played on other instruments.
   Name the first one you hear.
   Name the second.
   What happens when the theme is repeated on the second instrument?
   What instrument is added?
To what family do these three instruments belong?
Describe the tone colour or **timbre** of each one.
Discuss which instrument you think is most suitable for this piece of music. Why?

LIP BEATS

Percussion instruments make music exciting.
Consonants give percussive sounds to speech.
Stress the **consonant sounds** as you say these rhythms:

Doo bah   pa sha-ba sha-ba bee-bah   pa cha

Kee pa but-ton doo bah   sha boom   sha

Make the chant sound like percussion instruments.
Leave out the vowel sounds. Try to say it without
letting air escape.

Drums talk too. Experiment with a drum. Find
ways to "say" the chant.

    Try — fingertips
        — flat fingers
        — palms

    Strike — the rim
           — the head near the rim
           — the centre

How can you use both hands?

Make up your own rhythms.

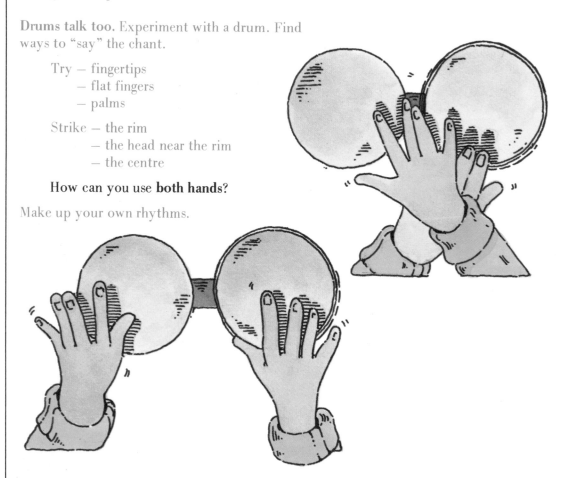

BONGO JOE

Rote Song

Composer Unknown

Hear the mu - sic with the bon - go beat. It's

com-ing from the house at the end of the street. For there lives

Bon - go Joe with his drums so grand, and he's the

best bon - go play - er in all of the land.

Create a **bongo rondo.**

Use the song as the A section.
Whisper this chant as part of your other sections:

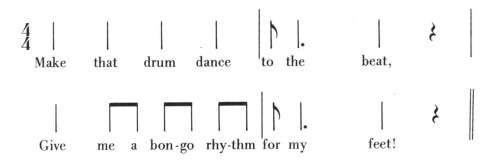

Make that drum dance to the beat,

Give me a bon-go rhy-thm for my feet!

Take turns improvising bongo rhythms during the chant.

FOUR WHITE HORSES

Rote Song

American Folk Song

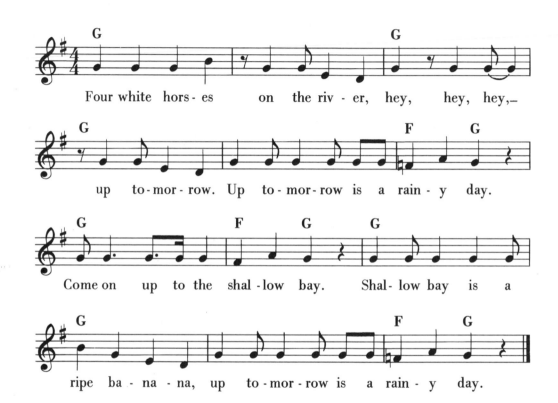

G: d m s m d   1 2 3 sing

G ... **G**
Four white hors-es   on the riv-er, hey,   hey, hey,—

G ... **F** **G**
up to-mor-row. Up to-mor-row is a rain-y day.

G ... **F** **G** **G**
Come on   up to the shal-low bay.   Shal-low bay is a

G ... **F** **G**
ripe ba-na-na, up to-mor-row is a rain-y day.

Play the game. Work in fours. Face your partner.

Clap right hands,
then left hands:

Clap your neigh-
bour's hands:

Switch levels. Continue alternating levels as you repeat the song.

SPRING

COME BE MERRY

Note/Rote Song and Round

Composer Unknown/Additional Lyrics by P. Brooks

G: d m s m d s, 1 2 3 sing

Brightly

Come be mer - ry, dance and sing! Wel - come in the hap - py— spring.

a little slower

Win - ter days are fad - ing fast, warm winds blow-ing, skies o'er-cast.

Birds are re-turn - ing to the glen. Green buds dress the trees once a-gain.

a tempo

Come be mer - ry, dance and sing! Wel - come in the hap - py— spring.

Step this rhythm
as you sing:

Once you know the rhythmic steps, form a circle.
Discover ways to show the **ABA form**
of the song with other movements.

116

TODAY

Note/Rote Song

Randy Sparks

F: d m s, m d s,   1 2 3 1 sing

Tempo can help express the **meaning** of a song.
Follow the tempo markings as you sing.

Adagio   *ritardando*   *a tempo*

Adagio

To - day   while the blos - soms   still   cling   to   the   vine,

I'll   taste   your   straw - ber - ries,   I'll   drink   your   sweet   wine.

a tempo

A   mil - lion   to - mor - rows   shall   all   pass   a - way

rit.

Ere   I   for - get   all   the   joys   that   are   mine   to - day.

117

NEW SHOES

Note/Rote Song

M. Suddaby and N. Boudreau

Eb: d' s m d s,   1 2 3 4 1 2 3 sing

Read the rhythm of the following chant. Snap your fingers on all the rests.

4/4

Sparx,   Ni - ke,   Cou - gars,   Brooks.

Cen - ti - pedes in shoe stores get might - y   fun - ny looks!

Run - ners aren't the on - ly shoes that cen - ti - pedes   buy,

Boots   and muk - luks   keep their toot - sies dry.

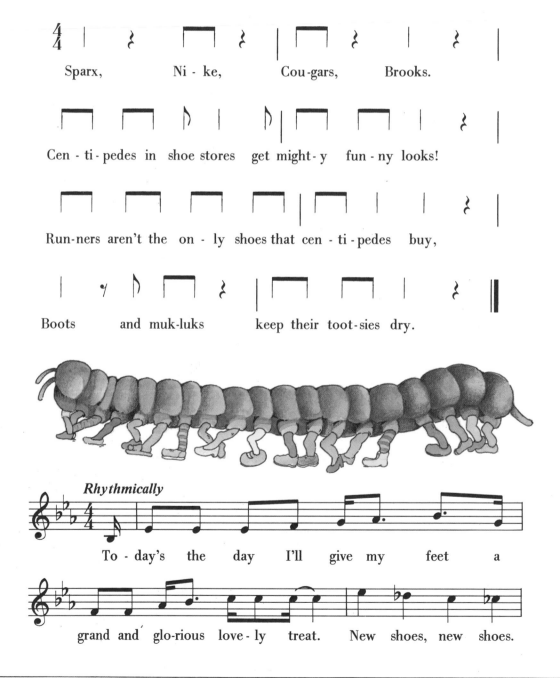

Rhythmically

To - day's   the   day   I'll give my   feet   a

grand and glo - rious love - ly treat. New shoes, new shoes.

They'll feel just right! I think I'll wear 'em to bed to-night.

𝄋 Chorus

Clap your hands. Slap your hips. Roll your eyes. Smack your lips.

Fine

Tap your toes. Shout "hoo-ray!" I'm gon-na get new shoes to-day!

Slower

My poor lit-tle feet are oh so sad. My worn out shoes have

got so bad, The tongue is torn, the lac-es ripped,

D.S. al Fine

the soles so worn they slip____ and slip.____

When you know the song,
divide into two groups for the chorus.

Group 1 sings the chorus twice.
Group 2 whispers the chant.

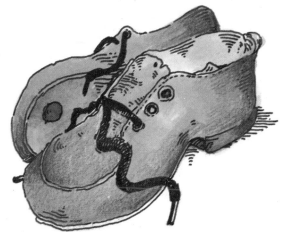

THE BIRDS' COURTING SONG

Note/Rote Song

American

Fm(Ab): d t, l, d m d   1 2 1   sing

1. "Hi!" says the black - bird sit - ting on a chair,
2. "Hi!" says the lit - tle leath - er winged bat,

"Once I court - ed a la - dy fair; She proved fick - le and
"I'll tell you the ___ rea - son that, the rea - son that ___ I

turned her back, And ev - er since then I've dressed in black."
fly by night Is be - cause I lost my heart's de - light." ___

Chorus

Tow - dy, ow - dy, did - dle do - dum, Tow - dy, ow - dy, did - dle do - day,

Tow - dy, ow - dy, did - dle do - dum, Tow - dy, ow - dy, did - dle do - day.

3. "Hi!" says the little mourning dove,
"I'll tell you how to regain her love;
Court her night and court her day,
Never give her time to say 'Oh, nay.'"

4. "Hi!" says the blue jay, as she flew,
"If I was a young man I'd have two,
If one proved fickle and chanced for to go
I'd have a new string to my bow."

5. "Hi!" says the woodpecker, sitting on the fence,
"Once I courted a handsome wench.
She proved fickle and from me fled,
And ever since then my head's been red."

I SING TO THE STARS

Poem

Nancy Prasad/Arr. by Nancy Telfer

Divide into four groups. Each group will perform one section — A, B, C or D.

A: Say this poem to the rhythms shown:

I sing to the stones and the sea and the sky

I sing to the lost ones, the child I hear cry.

I sing to the smoke-stacks, sub - ways and street - cars,

And when it is night, I sing to the stars.

B: Create your own melody using these rhythms. Sing to "ah."
Make it sound like you're singing to "the stones and the sea and the sky."

A: Repeat **A** but this time whisper it.

C: Sing this quietly:

I sing —— to the lost ones, the child —— I hear cry.

A: Repeat **A** *mf*.

D: Create your own percussion part.
Make it sound like "the smoke-stacks, subways and street cars."

A: Repeat **A** with all four groups saying the poem loudly.

121

WHO CAN SAIL?

Rote Song

Swedish Folk Song/English Lyrics Adapted by R. Fenn

B7   Em

shed   not   a   sin - gle   tear?_____
shed   not   a   sin - gle   tear._____

Many pieces, like this one, begin and end on the **I chord**.
Match the chord numbers to the chord names above the notes.

LISTENING:

"Mystery Composition"

Hugh LeCaine

Styles change with time. **Modern music** sounds different from music of the last century or earlier. What other things change style over a period of time?

Listen to this twentieth-century Canadian piece.

What makes it sound **modern**?
Can you hear melodies? rhythm patterns?

This piece was created using one single sound.

What do you think the sound was?
How is it altered?
How could the piece have been created?

Choose a title for this composition.
Ask your teacher for its real name.

SOUND PICTURES

Nancy Telfer

Discovery Page

If these pictures became sounds, what would they sound like?

Try:

percussion

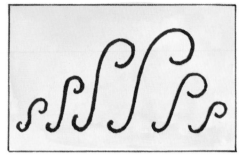

mouth sounds

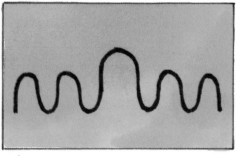

voice

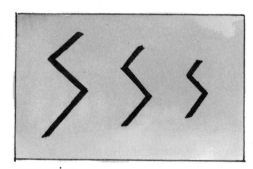

percussion

environmental sounds

Each picture could be interpreted in many different ways!

Choose a class conductor.
Divide the class into five groups.
Give each group a picture to express in sound.

Each group should:
— decide how the picture would sound
— practise the sounds several times

The conductor will direct all the groups together using the sound score below. The conductor will point to each group showing when it should begin and end. Each group will repeat its sound until the conductor signals it to stop.

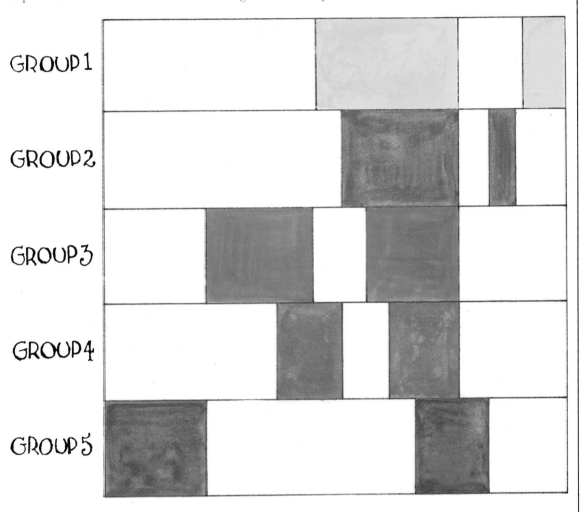

Where is the climax?
Decide where you would like it **soft** or **loud**.
Perform it again using these **dynamics**.

AU CHANT DE L'ALOUETTE

Note/Rote Song

French Folk Song/English Lyrics by M. Trotter

Em(G): *d t, l, d m d l, s,*   1   2   sing

Chorus

Au   chant   de   l'a - lou - et - te   je   veille   et   je   dors,

1.   2.   *Fine*

J'é - cou - te   l'a - lou - ette   et   puis   je   m'en   dors.   dors.

Verse

1. Si - len - tly   the   sun   melts from   the   sky,
2. Nes - tled   in   his   nest   is the lit - tle   thrush,
3. Na - ture tucks   her   dear   ones in - to   their   beds,

Lov - ing - ly   the   sun   says a fond good - bye,
Vil - lag - es   and   towns   slow their dai - ly   rush,
Si - lent - ly   the   dew   her soft blan - ket   spreads,

D.C. al Fine

Gen - tly   the world   hums   its   lul - la - by.
O - ver   hill   and   dale   falls   a   gen - tle   hush.
What   a   love - ly   peace   the___   eve - ning   sheds.

Draw a phrase map of the song as you sing. How many phrases are there?

How many phrases sound **finished**? Put a period after the phrases that come to rest.

How many phrases sound **unfinished**? Put a question mark after them.

SPRING FESTIVALS

In Japan, children celebrate the arrival of spring with a big kite festival.

In India, children paint each other red. The game, called *holi*, gets even messier. They shoot coloured water at each other with squirt guns.

In Mittenwald, Germany, men in ugly masks scare winter away on Crazy Thursday. Later in the day they welcome spring's arrival by parading in smiling masks and ringing bells.

In England, a celebration is held on May Day. People gather flowers, dress in special clothes and perform morris or maypole dances.

Spring festivals are held all over the world.

CONSTANT BILLY

Note/Rote Song

Traditional

G: *d m s m s d*   1 2 1 sing

"Constant Billy" is a morris dance tune. Costumed dancers work in sets of six. They perform one basic step as they trace patterns, called figures, on the floor. The figures are different for each verse. The chorus figure is always the same.

Sticks or scarves add excitement to the dance. Pipes, drums and other instruments, such as violins or accordions, accompany the song.

Sing the song as you walk in a circle. Learn the dance.

G   D7   G   C

Oh, my Bil - ly, my con - stant Bil - ly, When will I see my

D7   G   **Chorus** G   C   D7   G

Bil - ly a - gain?   Bil - ly a - gain,   Bil - ly a - gain,

G   C   D7   G   G

Bil - ly a - gain,   Bil - ly a - gain,   Oh, my Bil - ly, my

D7   G   C   D7   G

con - stant Bil - ly, When will I see my Bil - ly a - gain?

DRESS THE PART

Make your own costumes. All members of your group should choose the same colours.

Shoulder Sashes
Cut two strips of cloth or crepe
paper 4 cm by 130 cm. Wear them
over a white shirt. Put one strip
over each shoulder and fasten it at
your waist, under the opposite arm.
Pin ribbon or narrow strips of
paper where the sashes cross in
front and back. Add more ribbons
at your cuff, shoulders and upper
sleeve.

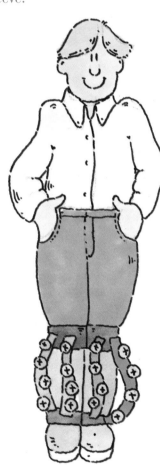

Shin Bells
Tuck your pant legs into knee socks.
Measure your calf just below your
knee and above your ankle. For
each place, cut waistband elastic
2.5 cm larger than your measure-
ment. Join the ends of each piece to
form circles. Slip them onto your
leg. Cut three strong ribbons to run
up from the ankle to knee elastic.
Sew a few bells along each ribbon.
Wear your shin bells while you
dance.

Sticks
Make all sticks 80 cm long.
Cut them from old broom handles.

Decorate a hat with ribbons and
spring flowers.

LISTENING:

Primitive people welcomed spring too. Stravinsky's *Rite of Spring*
is a sound painting of this celebration. It is the music for a ballet.
The section you will hear is "Dance of the Young People." How does
the music express their wild, untamed nature? For clues, listen to the
— **beats** and **accents**
— **melodies**
— instrument colours, or **timbres**

Follow these **melodies** in the air when you hear them:

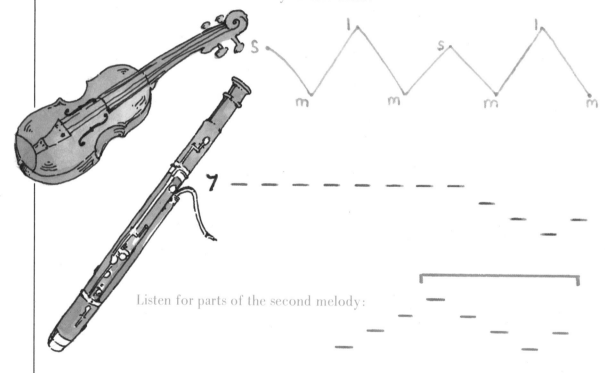

Listen for parts of the second melody:

Show these **beats** silently when you hear them.
Can you show the **accents** silently too?

Compare this dance with the morris dance "Constant Billy."
How does the music of each make you feel?

BARBERSHOP DAYS

Barbershop singing became popular around the turn
of the century. Groups of people, usually men,
gathered together to sing songs in **four-part harmony**.
The singing became known as "barbershop" because
they often met to practice while getting their weekly
haircut and shave. Many of the songs are still popular
today. Some of them are in this unit.

A BICYCLE BUILT FOR TWO

Note/Rote Song

Harry Dacre

G: d m s m s   1 2 3 1 2 sing

Barbershop songs have **four-part harmony** that sounds different from what we usually sing. The **unique sound** is created partly because the melody isn't in the highest voice. The melody, or **lead**, is sung by the **second-highest** voice, with the tenor above and baritone and bass parts below.

In this song and others in this section, the lead and tenor parts are taken from barbershop arrangements. The lead is usually the lower of the two parts.

In waltz time

1. Dai - sy,   Dai - sy,   give me your an - swer, do.___

I'm   half   cra - zy,   all for the love   of   you.___

It won't be   a styl - ish mar - riage!___ I can't af-ford   a   car - riage,___

But you'll look sweet up - on   the seat   of a bi - cy - cle built for two.___

2. Henry, Henry, this is my answer true.
I'm not crazy over the likes of you.
If you can't afford a carriage,
forget about the marriage,
I won't be jammed,
I won't be crammed on a bicycle built for two.

PREPARE FOR ACTION!

People who sing barbershop songs usually do it just for the fun of making music—often improvising as they go along.

They also add actions to their singing. They enjoy performing for other people and try to be as entertaining as possible.

You can try some barbershop actions with some of the songs you're learning.

Sways are used when the chords change.

Spreads are used for endings.

You can also use actions that show the word meanings.

YES, SIR, YOU'RE MY BABY

Rote Song

G. Kahn and W. Donaldson/Arr. by M. Trotter and B. Charlton

C: *d m s d' s———m*   1   2   3   sing

Try some **barbershop actions** when you've learned this song. You may want to try adding some props like canes or hats to help you tell the story.

Yes, sir, you're my ba - by, No, sir, I don't mean may - be,

Yes, sir, you're my ba - by now. (my ba - by)

now.——— By the way, (by the way) by the way, (by the way)

e - ven when you're grown up I'll say: (I'll say it)

C   G7

"Yes, sir, you're my ba - by, No, sir, I don't mean may - be,

G7   C

Yes, sir, you're my ba - by now. (and how)

F   F7

And when you turn __ fif - ty, I think that you'll be nif - ty.

C   C♯7

You'll still be my ba - by, e - ven when you're eight - y. Yes,

D7   F   G7   C F C

you (or a hun-dred and two) are my ba - by now. Yes, sir!

O MISTER MOON

Rote Song

Traditional

Ab: *d m s m d s,*   1 2 3 4 1 2 sing

When singing in competitions, barbershoppers are judged on different skills. Most important is how well their voices sound together in harmony and whether they have **stage presence.** Stage presence is a poised, confident way of looking and acting on stage.

Add actions to this song.

How confident and enthusiastic can you be?
How well do you do your actions as a group?
Do the actions you choose fit the song well?

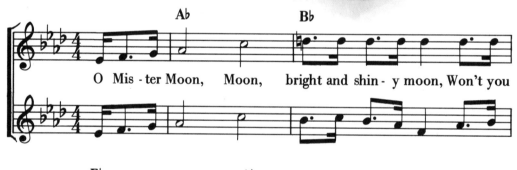

O Mis - ter Moon, Moon, bright and shin - y moon, Won't you

please shine down on me?____ O Mis - ter Moon, Moon,

bright and shin - y moon, Won't you come from be - hind that tree?

136

Unison

A♭

Oh, my life's in dan - ger but I'm scared to run; There's a

D♭7   A♭

man be - hind me with a big shot - gun. O Mis - ter Moon, Moon,

B♭   E♭   E♭7

bright and shin - y moon, Won't you please shine down on,

E♭   E♭7 E♭7   A♭

please shine down on,   please shine down on   me?_____

MISTRESS SHADY

Rote Song

Traditional

Bb: d m s m d s, 1 2 sing

You'll find many accidentals in these songs because **V7** and **minor chords** are so common in barbershop music.

In the early days of barbershop, people used to get together to have fun trying out new harmony parts. Many barbershop arrangements developed from this practice, which was called "woodshedding."

Try improvising some harmony for the first part of this song.

Oh, Mis - tress Shad - y,＿＿＿ She is a la - dy,＿＿＿

＿＿＿ She has a daugh - ter＿＿＿ whom I a - dore.＿＿＿

＿＿＿ Each day I court her,＿＿＿ I mean the daugh - ter,＿＿

＿＿ Ev - 'ry Sunday, Monday, Tuesday, Wednesday, Thursday, Friday,

Sat - ur-day, Sun-day aft - er-noon at half - past four.＿＿＿

138

STAY WITH ME

Note/Rote Song

Heather Conkie

1. Cloud - y mists and sum - mer show - ers, won't you please come
2. Rock - y shores and paint - ed flow - ers stretch as far as

light on me? Love the grass and paint the flow - ers,
you can see. They love the mist and sum - mer show - ers,

in a dew - y tap - es - try._____ And the
won't you please come stay with me?_____ And the

riv - er makes its wind - ing pas - sage to the sea, And the
riv - er makes its stead - y pas - sage to the sea, And the

sky is all a - lone with you and me._____ And the
sky will al - ways be with you and me._____

A **flat** ♭ lowers the pitch of a note one-half step, or **semitone**. Once a note is lowered, it remains that way through a whole measure, unless it is cancelled by a **natural** ♮ .

How many **accidentals** can you find?

How many **flat notes** will you sing?

OVER THE RAINBOW

Rote Song

H. Arlen and E. Harburg

D: d m s d' s m d   1   2   1   sing

This music was written for the film *The Wizard of Oz*. The main character, Dorothy, was originally played by Judy Garland, a well-known child actress who made the song a hit.

Follow the tempo markings and choose dynamics to give expression to the lyrics.

Moderato

Some - where o - ver the rain - bow, way up high,

There's a land that I heard of once in a lull - a - by.

Some - where o - ver the rain - bow skies are blue,

And the dreams that you dare to dream real-ly do come true. Some-

dreamily

day I'll wish up - on a star and wake up where the clouds are far be -

hind me,_____ Where trou - bles melt like lem - on drops, a -

way a - bove the chim - ney tops, that's where you'll find me.

Some - where o - ver the rain - bow blue - birds fly,

Birds fly o - ver the rain - bow, why, then, oh, why can't

1.
2.
3

I? I?

If hap - py lit - tle blue - birds fly be -

rit.

yond the rain - bow, why, oh, why can't I?

JINGLE, JANGLE, JINGLE

Note/Rote Song

J.J. Lilley and F. Loesser

Eb: d m s m d l, s,   1 2 sing

Refrain

I got spurs that jin - gle, jan - gle, jin - gle,_____

As I go rid - in' mer - ri - ly a - long._____

And they sing, "Oh, ain't you glad you're sin - gle!"_____

Fine

And that song ain't so ver - y far from wrong._____

Verse

1. Oh, Sal - ly Jane,_____ Oh, Sal - ly Jane,_____
2. Oh, Bes - sie Lou,_____ Oh, Bes - sie Lou,_____

Oh, Sal - ly Jane,   Oh, Sal - ly Jane,
Oh, Bes - sie Lou,   Oh, Bes - sie Lou,

D.C. al Fine

Though I'd love to stay for - ev - er, This is why I can't re - main,
Though we'd done a heap of dream - in', This is why it won't come true,

LAREDO

Rote Song

American Folk Song/Arr. by M. Hoffman

F: d m s m d s,   1 2 3 4 1 2 sing

Smoothly

1. I'm off for La - re - do, fare - well my love; I'm
2. So prom - ise that you will wait for the day that

sor - ry to leave, 'tis true;   I will re - turn to you.

Chorus

I give you a key of
To lock up your heart for-

sil - ver, my love, at - tached to a gold - en chain;
ev - er, my love, 'til I can re - turn a - gain.

Compare this song to "Jingle, Jangle, Jingle" on page 142.
Consider **form**, **rhythm**, **harmony** and **mood**.

GOOD-BYE AND A BYE-BYE

Note/Rote Song

American

G: *d m s m s*   1 2 3 sing

Find measures that are the same; different.

Go - ing down to Cai - ro, good - bye and a bye - bye.

Go - ing down to Cai - ro, good - bye, Li - za Jane.

Slap them boots and make them shine, good - bye and a bye - bye.

Slap them boots and make them shine, good - bye, Li - za Jane.

Do the dance.

In partners, form a double circle. As you sing, **promenade** left to the end of bar four. On the word "Slap," shake right hands with your partner, pass right shoulders and extend your left hand to the new friend facing you. **Grand chain** and repeat the song till you meet your partner. **Promenade** to the end of the song.

144

SUMMER SPORTS

P. Brooks

Poem

I love summer,
  because . . .
      Bats crack,
      Racquets smash,
      Joggers pant,
      Swimmers splash,
      Wheels whirr,
      Frisbees whizz,
Summer sport sounds,
Sound GREAT!

Add an accompaniment to the poem:

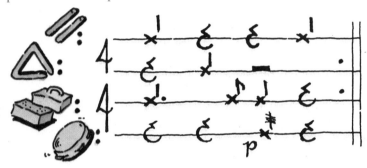

Create "variations on a theme."

Think of ways to alter the middle section of the poem.

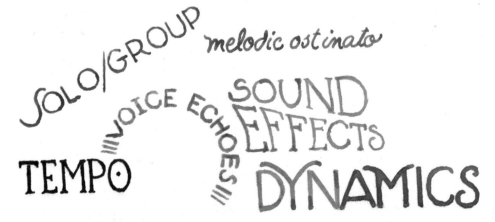

Choose three or four variations to develop a longer poem.

THE THREE "NOTS"

Note/Rote Song

Chinese Folk Song/English Lyrics by M. Trotter

G: *d* *m* *s* *m*   1   2   1   sing

For the people of Kwei Cho, the beautiful mountain province of China, life holds three "nots." This song voices their humorous complaint.

1. Peo - ple on our moun-tain high__ live__ with three nots 'til__ they die:
2. Though we love our moun-tain high,__ some days we long to__ be__ dry.
3. Emp - ty is the moun-tain breeze,__ life__ is__ hard with rocks and trees.

Though our streams and slopes a - bound, not__ three miles are on__ flat ground.
Though we dream of sun - ny plains, not__ three days pass with - out__ rain.
We've been poor since time be - gan,__ not__ three cents has an - y__ man.

Coda after v. 3

Ke tong ke tong tong tong, Ke tong ke tong tong tong   Ke tong ke tong tong tong

146

ZUM GALI GALI

Rote Song

Hebrew Folk Song

G: d m s m d   1 2 sing

This **work song** tells of the pioneers, the *halutzim*, who created farms in the barren Israeli desert. Strong rhythms are common in work songs of many lands.

1. *He-cha-lutz le-man a-vo-dah;___ A-vo-dah le-man he-cha-lutz.*
2. *A-vo-dah le-man he-cha-lutz;___ He-cha-lutz le-man a-vo-dah.*
3. *Ha-sha-lom le-man ha-'a-mim;___ Ha-'a-mim le-man ha-sha-lom.*

Use this ostinato while you sing.
Use it as an **introduction** and **interlude** too.

Zum ga-li ga-li ga-li, zum ga-li ga-li.

SHALOM CHAVERIM

Note Song and Round

Hebrew

Em(G): d t, l, d m d l, m,   1 2 3 4 1 2 sing

Sha-lom cha-ve-rim, sha-lom cha-ve-rim, sha-lom, sha-lom.
Fare-well, good friend, fare-well, good friend, fare-well, fare-well.

L'-hit-ra-ot, l'-hit-ra-ot, sha-lom, sha-lom.
Till we meet a-gain, till we meet a-gain, fare-well, fare-well.

EDELWEISS

Rote Song

Music by Richard Rodgers/Lyrics by Oscar Hammerstein

Bb: d' s m d m 1 2 3 1 2 sing

What is a **Broadway musical**? This song is from *The Sound of Music* by Rodgers and Hammerstein, a well-known writing team. What story does the musical tell?

O CANADA

Rote Song

Music by C. Lavalée/Lyrics by A. Routhier/English trans. by R. Weir

O Can - a - da! Our home and na - tive land,
O Ca - na - da! Ter - re de nos aï - eux,

True pa - triot love in all our sons com - mand.
Ton front est ceint de fleu - rons glo - ri - eux!

With glow - ing hearts we see thee rise,
Car ton bras sait por - ter l'é - pé - e,

The True North strong and free! From far and wide,
Il sait por - ter la croix! Ton his - toire est une

O Can - a - da, we stand on guard for thee.
é - po - pé - e des plus bril - lants ex - ploits.

God keep our land glo - rious and free!
Et ta va - leur, de foi trem - pée,

O Can - a - da, we stand on guard for thee.
Pro - té - ge - ra nos foy - ers et nos droits,

O Can - a - da, we stand on guard for thee.
Pro - té - ge - ra nos foy - ers et nos droits.

NOTE · REST VALUES · HAND SIGNS

doh'

ti

Common Time ($\frac{2}{4}$ $\frac{3}{4}$ $\frac{4}{4}$ ¢)

Note	Symbol	Rest	Name	Value (Beats in $\frac{4}{4}$ time)
𝅝	𝅝	▬	Whole	4
𝅗𝅥.	𝅗𝅥.	▬	Dotted half	3
𝅗𝅥	𝅗𝅥	▬	Half	2
♩.	|.	𝄽.	Dotted quarter	1½
♩	|	𝄽	Quarter	1
♪	♩	𝄾	Eighth	½
♫	⊓	𝄾	Two eighths	1
♬	⊓	𝄿	Sixteenth	¼
♬♬	⊓⊓	𝄿	Four sixteenths	1

tah

lah

si

Syncopated Patterns:

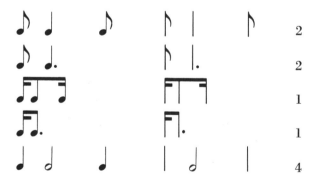

						Value
♪	♩		♪	|	♩	2
♪	♩.		♩	|.		2
♫	♩		⊓	⊓		1
♫.			⊓.			1
♩	𝅗𝅥	♩	|	𝅗𝅥	|	4

soh

fi

fah

Compound Time ($\frac{3}{8}$ $\frac{6}{8}$ $\frac{9}{8}$)

♪ = 1 beat

$\frac{6}{8}$ ♪ ♪ ♪ ♪ ♪ ♪   (Slow tempo)
      1   2   3   4   5   6

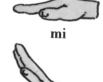

re

♩. = 1 beat

$\frac{6}{8}$ ♩.   ♩.   (Fast tempo)
     1   2

doh

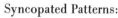

CHORDS FOR ACCOMPANYING SONGS

C major scale (no sharps or flats in key signature)

Letter names: C D E F G A B C

Syllables: d r m f s l t d'
Scale numbers: I II III IV V VI VII VIII

Chord names: C F G G7

Chord numbers: I IV V V7

I = d m s
IV = f l d'
V7 = s t r' f'

A minor scale (A minor is related to C major. They have the same key signature.)

Letter names: A B C D E F G♯ A

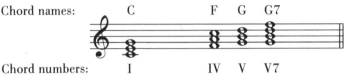

Syllables: l, t, d r m f si l
Scale numbers: I II III IV V VI VII VIII

Chord names: Am Dm E E7

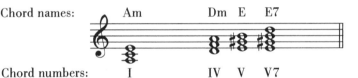

Chord numbers: I IV V V7

I = l, d m
IV = r f l
V7 = m si t r'

Other common chords are:

G major (one sharp)

G C D7

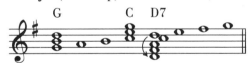

E minor (one sharp)

Em Am B7

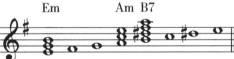

D major (two sharps)

D G A7

B minor (two sharps)

Bm Em F♯7

F major (one flat)

F B♭ C7

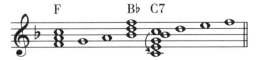

D minor (one flat)

Dm G♯m A7

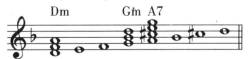

ACKNOWLEDGEMENTS

Care has been exercised to trace ownership of copyright material contained in this text. The publishers will gladly receive information that will enable them to rectify any reference or credit in subsequent editions.

Pg. 10 WHAT SOUND DO YOU HEAR? by Emily Hearn. First published in "Kites and Cartwheels" Nelson/Canada 1972. Permission granted by the author. Pg. 11 TEACH ME Lyrics by John Sone and Music by Rudy Toth. Reprinted by permission of Rudy Toth. Pg. 12 THE OLD GO-HUNGRY HASH HOUSE From the P.J. Thomas Collection, in *Songs of the Pacific Northwest*, 1979. Pg. 15 DO NOT WEEP Reprinted by permission of Keith Bissell. Pg. 16 TEMPO, TEMPO, TEMPO, from PICK-A-LITTLE, TALK-A-LITTLE and GOODNIGHT LADIES from "The Music Man" by Meredith Willson © 1957 FRANK MUSIC CORP. and RINIMER CORPORATION. International Copyright Secured. All Rights Reserved. Used By Permission. Pg. 22 INDEPENDENCE Excerpt from "Independence" from the musical "The Cabbagetown Kids" by Dodi Robb and Pat Patterson. Reprinted by permission of the composers. Pg. 27 HALLOWE'EN From THE LITTLE HILL, copyright 1949 by Harry Behn; copyright 1977 by Alice L. Behn. Reprinted by permission of Curtis Brown Ltd. Pg. 30 WITCHES From THIS IS MUSIC BOOK 5 by William Sur, Adeline McCall, William Fisher, Mary Tolbert. Copyright © 1967, 1971 by Allyn and Bacon, Inc. Used by permission. Pg. 31 NOVEMBER NIGHT From VERSE, by Adelaide Crapsey. Copyright 1922 by Algernon S. Crapsey and renewed 1950 by The Adelaide Crapsey Foundation. Reprinted by permission of Alfred A. Knopf, Inc. Pg. 32 HE'S GOT THE WHOLE WORLD IN HIS HANDS Arrangement © Copyright 1974 by The Presbyterian Church in Canada, 50 Wynford Dr., Don Mills, Ont. Canada. Pg. 45 SOFIA Words from MAKING MUSIC YOUR OWN 6, © 1965, 1971 General Learning Corporation. Reprinted by permission of Silver Burdett Company. Pg. 48 O HANUKAH Courtesy of Behrman House Inc. N.Y., N.Y. Pg. 52 GOD REST YOU MERRY, GENTLEMEN Arranged by: John Cacavas © 1963, 1965 WARNER BROS. INC. All Rights Reserved. Used by Permission. Pg. 56 CALYPSO CAROL Reprinted with the permission of Bosworth & Co. Ltd. 14/18 Heddon Street, London W1R 8DP. Pg. 58 IN THE TOWN From SAILORS AND SUNSHINE by Earle Terry, Lloyd H. Slind and Frank Churchley. Copyright © McGraw-Hill Ryerson Limited, 1974. Reprinted by permission. Pg. 64 THE HURON CAROL Reprinted by permission of Frederick Harris Music Co. Ltd. Pg. 65 THIS LAND, CANADA by Jo and Rudy Toth. From the record "Canada: A Young People's Musical Tour of Canada's Provinces and Territories" Reprinted by permission of Rudy Toth. Pg. 66 CANADA BLUES Traditional U.S. Folk Blues, originally titled THE CITY BLUES by Jerry Silverman, arranged by Jerry Silverman. Used by permission. Pg. 68 MACKENZIE RIVER Lyrics by Dick Halhed and Music by Ricky Hyslop. Reprinted by permission. Pg. 72 SQUID-JIGGIN' GROUND by A. R. Scammell © 1958 BMI CANADA assigned to Berandol Music Limited. International Copyright Secured. All Rights Reserved. Used by permission. Pg. 73 FORTY BELOW From the collection of Jon Bartlett and Rika Ruebsaat. Pg. 78 CAPE BRETON DREAM First Published by Breakwater Books Ltd. St. John's, Nfld. © 1978. Pg. 80 SASKATCHEWAN BLUES by Alison Pirot. Reprinted by permission. Pg. 83 SNOW Reprinted by permission of Holt, Rinehart and Winston, Publishers, Inc. N.Y., N.Y. Pg. 83 WINTER NIGHT Words by Charles Winter. From Songtime 6 by Holt, Rinehart and Winston of Canada, Ltd. Reprinted by permission of Charles Winter. Pg. 86 VALENTINE SWING Music & Lyrics by Brian D. Strachan. Reprinted by permission of Brian Strachan. Pg. 88 IT'S A SMALL WORLD © 1963 Wonderland Music Company, Inc. Words & Music by Richard M. & Robert B. Sherman. Pg. 96 MINKA Reprinted by permission of Holt, Rinehart & Winston, Publishers, Inc., N.Y., N.Y. Pg. 98 LINSTEAD MARKET by Louise Bennett for "Linstead Market" from *Jamaican Folk Songs* recorded by Folkways Records, N.Y. Pg. 100 MACARONI Reprinted with permission of Holt, Rinehart & Winston, Publishers, Inc., N.Y., N.Y. Pg. 103 THE BIRCH TREE From BASIC GOALS IN MUSIC 6. Copyright © McGRAW-HILL RYERSON LIMITED, 1975. Reprinted by permission. Pg. 105 WIND SONG by Lilian Moore, "Wind Song," (Copyright © 1966 by Scholastic Magazines, Inc.) in *I Feel the Same Way*. Copyright © 1967 by Lilian Moore (New York: Atheneum, 1967) Reprinted with the permission of Atheneum Publishers. Pg. 108 THE SYNCOPATED CLOCK Composer/Arranger: Leroy Anderson, Mitchell Parish Copyright © 1950 by Mills Music, Inc. Copyright renewed. Used with permission. All rights reserved. Pg. 114 FOUR WHITE HORSES Lois Choksy, THE KODALY CONTEXT: Creating an Environment for Musical Learning, © 1981, pp. 233-235. Adapted by permission of Prentice-Hall, Inc. Englewood Cliffs, N.J. Pg. 117 TODAY by Randy Sparks Copyright © 1964 Metro-Goldwyn-Mayer, Inc. Rights throughout the world controlled by Miller Music Corporation. By arrangement with Heritage House. All rights reserved. Used by permission. Pg. 118 NEW SHOES by Nan Boudreau & Marjorie Suddaby. Used with permission of the composers. Pg. 121 I SING TO THE STARS by Nancy Prasad. Reprinted by permission of the author. Pg. 134 YES, SIR, YOU'RE MY BABY Words by Gus Kahn, Music by Walter Donaldson. © Copyright 1925 Bourne Co., N.Y., N.Y., used by permission of Bourne Music Canada Limited, a division of Gordon V. Thompson Limited, 29 Birch Avenue, Toronto, Ontario, M4V 1E2. Original title YES SIR, THAT'S MY BABY. Pg. 136 O MISTER MOON From *Growing with Music, Book 6*, Wilson et al. (Englewood Cliffs, N.J.: Prentice-Hall, Inc.) 1968 (Canadian ed.). Pg. 139 STAY WITH ME Music and lyrics by Heather M. Conkie. Reprinted by permission. Pg. 140 OVER THE RAINBOW by E.Y. Harburg and Harold Arlen. Copyright © 1938, 1939, renewed 1966, 1967 Metro-Goldwyn-Mayer, Inc. All rights administered and controlled by LEO FEIST, INC. All rights reserved. Used by permission. Pg. 142 JINGLE, JANGLE, JINGLE Music: Frank Loesser/Words: Joseph J. Lilley. Copyright 1942 by Paramount Music Corp. Copyright renewed 1969. Used by permission of Chappell Canada. Pg. 143 LAREDO From SILVER BURDETT MUSIC 8. © 1982 Silver Burdett Company. Arranged by Mary E. Hoffman. Reprinted by permission. Pg 147 SHALOM CHAVERIM Music Traditional. Arranged by Naomi Stewart. Translated by Eleanor Chroman. © Instructor. Used By Permission. Pg. 148 EDELWEISS Words by Oscar Hammerstein 2nd/Music by Richard Rodgers. Copyright © 1959 by Richard Rodgers and Oscar Hammerstein 2nd. Williamson Music Inc., New York, N.Y. owner of publication and allied rights for all countries of the Western Hemisphere. International copyright secured. ALL RIGHTS RESERVED. Pg. 149 O CANADA National Anthem Published under authority of the Speaker of the House of Commons, Ottawa, K1A 0A6.

PHOTO CREDITS: pg. 19 "Return from the Harvest Field" by Aurele de Foy Suzor-Cote. From the Collection of the National Gallery of Canada, Ottawa. Pg. 41 "Family and Rainstorm" by David Alexander Colville. From the Collection of the National Gallery of Canada, Ottawa. Pg. 110 (Left) "Skidegate—Oil on Canvas" by Emily Carr. From the Collection of the Vancouver Art Gallery (42.3.48) Photo by Jim Gorman/Vancouver Art Gallery. (Right) "Skidegate (1912) Oil on Board" by Emily Carr. From the Collection of the Vancouver Art Gallery (42.3.46) Photo by Robert Keziere/Vancouver Art Gallery.

CLASSIFIED INDEX

ALPHABETICAL INDEX